Contemporary Systems Thinking

Series Editors

Gianfranco Minati, Italian Systems Society, Milano, Italy

Alessandro Giuliani, Department of Mathematics and Physics, Università Roma Tre, Rome, Italy

Leonardo Bich, IAS Research Centre, University of the Basque Country, Leioa, Spain

Contemporary Systems Thinking is a series of texts focusing on interdisciplinary approaches, concepts, and issues of systems science and systems thinking (systemics). Texts in this series are not discursive but rather academic and scientific. Popular topics in the series include complexity, connectionism, chaos and emergence, as they are related to disciplinary systemics, theoretical systemics, applied systemics, and cultural systemics. Special consideration is given to texts about contemporary social issues that have predominant systemic aspects, such as climate, ecology, energy, public health, business, and others.

Kay-Yut Chen

The Social and Economic Behavior of AI Agents

Theory and Experiments

Springer

Kay-Yut Chen
Information Systems and Operations Management
University of Texas at Arlington
Arlington, TX, USA

ISSN 1568-2846
Contemporary Systems Thinking
ISBN 978-3-032-18065-0 ISBN 978-3-032-18066-7 (eBook)
https://doi.org/10.1007/978-3-032-18066-7

This Springer imprint is published by the registered company Springer Nature Switzerland AG
The registered company address is: Gewerbestrasse 11, 6330 Cham, Switzerland

Acknowledgments The persona engineering techniques framework discussed in Chapter 3, Section 3.6.2 was developed in collaboration with Jingguo Wang, Yan Lang and Jingjie Su for a forthcoming paper. I am grateful for the discussions that helped refine this conceptual framework.

The spherical coordinate descent procedure presented in Chapter 4, Section 4.4.2 was originally developed in collaboration with Shan Li for different research purposes. I thank her for the discussions on this computational methodology, which I have adapted for the trait measurement framework in this work.

I gratefully acknowledge the use of AI tools in the preparation of this manuscript. Claude (Anthropic) and ChatGPT (OpenAI) were used for copy-editing, LaTeX coding, coding assistance for experiment implementation and data analysis, and providing opinions about expositions. All research design, data collection, analysis, interpretation, and substantive intellectual content remain my original work.

I am grateful to the College of Business, University of Texas at Arlington for providing the research environment and resources that made this work possible.

I thank the anonymous reviewers for their helpful comments.

Competing Interests The author has no competing interests to declare that are relevant to the content of this manuscript.

Contents

List of Figures

List of Tables

Chapter 1
Introduction

1.1 Overview

This book serves as both a research report on current findings and an urgent call-to-action for emerging research opportunities, while bearing witness to the remarkable transformation of artificial intelligence from mere tools to our companions and partners in decision-making. Understanding the social behaviors of AI systems has become increasingly critical as these technologies transition from isolated computational tools to integrated decision-making partners in human environments. As Dafoe et al. (2021) argue in their seminal work on cooperative AI, the capacity for machines to exhibit and understand social behaviors, including trust and cooperation, will fundamentally determine their effectiveness in multi-agent systems and human-AI collaborations. Without this social intelligence layer, even the most advanced AI systems may fail to align with human values and expectations in complex interactive settings.

As AI systems increasingly interact with each other and with humans in complex decision environments, their social and economic behaviors emerge as a critical area of study. An example of how economics and social behavior interact: in the trust game, one player decides how much money to send to another player, knowing the amount will be tripled, and the second player then decides how much to return. This simple scenario combines economic calculation (maximizing monetary payoffs) with social considerations (trust in the partner's reciprocity, fairness in sharing gains). Such environments, which we examine throughout this book, reveal how economic incentives and social behaviors intertwine in artificial systems. However, the landscape of AI interaction research is vast and multifaceted. This book deliberately narrows its focus to the intrinsic social and economic behaviors exhibited by AI systems themselves, rather than exploring the broader domains of AI-human interactions or human behavioral adaptations in response to AI. While these adjacent fields offer rich research opportunities, they introduce additional layers of complexity that would dilute our core analysis. By concentrating specifically on how AI

K. Chen, *The Social and Economic Behavior of AI Agents*, Contemporary Systems Thinking, https://doi.org/10.1007/978-3-032-18066-7_1

agents develop, express, and modify social behaviors like trust, cooperation, and strategic decision-making, we establish fundamental insights that inevitably inform those related domains. The behavioral patterns we uncover in autonomous AI systems will ultimately shape both how humans interact with these systems and how humans modify their own behaviors in response—making this focused approach a foundation for broader understanding in the field.

Research on AI behavioral patterns has grown rapidly in recent years. Published studies now examine AI capabilities across diverse contexts including repeated games (Akata et al., 2025), collective decision-making (Brewer et al., 2024), consumer preferences (Goli & Singh, 2024), trust behavior (Xie et al., 2024), and operations management (Chen et al., 2025), with findings appearing across multiple disciplines. The pace of research is evidenced by a substantial body of working papers currently under review. This book contributes to this emerging literature by examining behavioral patterns across different AI architectures and developing frameworks for systematic behavioral analysis.

The central question that drives our investigation is both fundamental and pragmatic: if AI systems can indeed exhibit human-like social behaviors, from cooperation and trust to competitive strategies and fairness judgments, what are the underlying mechanisms that generate these behaviors? This question leads us to examine two fundamentally different AI architectures with distinct behavioral origins. We focus on Deep Q-Networks (DQNs) and Large Language Models (LLMs) not merely as representative examples, but because they embody complementary pathways through which social behaviors can emerge in artificial systems. DQNs, with their capacity to learn directly from environmental feedback without prior knowledge, allow us to investigate how social behaviors can arise from algorithmic processes through reinforcement learning. LLMs, conversely, demonstrate how social behaviors can be inherited from human-generated data, reflecting cultural patterns embedded in text. These approaches mirror different aspects of human social capability development—direct experiential learning versus cultural absorption—and are being deployed in distinct but overlapping application domains. By examining both architectures, we can develop a more comprehensive understanding of the potential origins of social intelligence in AI systems and identify principles that may generalize across architectural differences. This dual approach is particularly valuable as AI systems increasingly participate in hybrid environments where both DQN-like and LLM-based agents may interact, requiring a unified framework for understanding social dynamics across architectural boundaries. Table 1.1 summarizes the key differences between these complementary approaches.

To effectively analyze the social and economic behaviors of AI systems, we must first establish a foundational understanding of the two primary architectures examined in this book: Deep Q-Networks and Large Language Models. The following two sections provide conceptual overviews of these technologies—not as programming guidelines or mathematical treatises, but as frameworks for understanding how different AI architectures can develop and express social behaviors. While we introduce some mathematical notation where necessary to clarify key relationships, our focus remains on building intuitions rather than detailed formulations. This conceptual

Table 1.1 Comparison of DQN-based and LLM-based agent approaches

Aspect	DQN-based agents	LLM-based agents
Knowledge source	Learned through direct interaction with environment	Pre-trained from vast corpus of human-written text
Memory structure	Explicitly programmed into architecture	Added through prompt design and context management
Generalizability	Limited to specifically trained environment	Transfers knowledge across diverse contexts
Training requirements	Game-specific, requires extensive iterations	General pre-training with minor task adaptation
Behavioral origins	Emergent from reinforcement learning process	Inherited from patterns in training data
Decision-making process	Value-based action selection optimizing future rewards	Pattern completion based on statistical regularities
Adaptability	Requires retraining for new environments	Can adapt to new scenarios through prompting

approach is deliberately chosen to make the material accessible to researchers across disciplines while providing sufficient technical grounding to appreciate the mechanisms through which social behaviors emerge in these systems. Additionally, we introduce the GPT-Language-based Experimental Economics System (GLEES), one systematic framework for creating, deploying, and studying LLM-based agents in economic and social game environments. GLEES represents a methodological bridge between traditional experimental economics and AI research, enabling controlled investigations of how LLM-based agents interact, make decisions, and potentially develop cooperative or competitive strategies across repeated interactions. While GLEES provides our primary experimental platform, we also examine findings from alternative implementations and external studies to provide a comprehensive view of LLM behavioral patterns across different experimental approaches.

Having established the technical foundations of Deep Q-Networks and Large Language Models, as well as the GLEES framework for agent simulation, we then examine how behavioral economics frameworks can be applied to understand these systems' social and economic behaviors. This introduction draws from the rich literature of behavioral economics, a field that has systematically documented and modeled deviations from purely rational economic behavior in humans through both experiments and theoretical modeling. The behavioral economics approach offers well-established experimental paradigms and analytical tools that can be applied to AI systems, allowing researchers to characterize AI behaviors in terms of risk preferences, fairness considerations, and other social dimensions already familiar to economists and psychologists. Throughout this analysis, we draw on multiple experimental implementations, including GLEES-based studies and other research, to build a comprehensive understanding of LLM behavioral characteristics. Beyond applying existing frameworks, we provide a discussion of several critical research design considerations specific to studying AI social behavior, including issues of reproducibility, the role of stochasticity in decision processes, appropriate benchmarking against human behavior, and methodological questions in attributing intentionality or preferences to AI systems. For LLM-based agents in particular, methodological challenges include prompt sensitivity, the non-learning nature of these systems during experiments, and the need for cross-model validation as model versions evolve. These methodological discussions are essential not only for interpreting current findings but also for considering rigorous approaches for future work at the intersection of artificial intelligence and behavioral science. Building on these empirical and methodological foundations, this book develops a mathematical framework for understanding AI behavioral patterns. Chapter 4 presents the Embedding-Based Trait Theory (EBTT), which formalizes the relationship between persona prompts and behavioral outcomes through semantic embeddings and trait measurement. The Reference-Anchored Trait Framework (RATF) within EBTT provides a systematic approach to quantifying and predicting behavioral characteristics in LLM-based agents across different decision contexts. The framework is accompanied by empirical validation using risk preference elicitation tasks and cross-task behavioral prediction.

The rest of this chapter is organized as follows. In Sect. 1.2, we examine the technical foundations of Deep Q-Networks (DQNs) and how their architecture enables the emergence of complex decision-making capabilities through reinforcement learning mechanisms. Section 1.3 introduces the GPT-Language-based Experimental Economics System (GLEES), a framework for creating and managing LLM-based agents in economic and social simulations, detailing its design principles and operational capabilities. Section 1.4 discusses the application of behavioral economics concepts to AI systems, outlining key experimental paradigms and analytical frameworks that can characterize AI social and economic behaviors. Finally, Sect. 1.5 explores critical research issues in this emerging field, with particular emphasis on emergent behaviors in multi-agent AI systems, reproducibility challenges, and methodological considerations for studying AI social dynamics. Throughout these sections, we maintain a conceptual focus that builds intuition while providing sufficient technical detail to support the analyses presented in subsequent chapters.

1.2 Deep Q-Network—A Primer

Deep neural networks represent a class of machine learning algorithms inspired by the structure and function of the human brain, capable of learning complex patterns from large amounts of data through multiple layers of interconnected nodes. While deep learning has transformed various domains including computer vision and natural language processing, its integration with reinforcement learning—a paradigm where agents learn by interacting with their environment—has opened new frontiers in artificial intelligence. The Deep Q-Network (DQN) approach, introduced by Mnih et al. (2015), marked a significant advancement by successfully combining deep learning with Q-learning, enabling AI systems to learn effective decision-making strategies directly from high-dimensional sensory inputs. This approach has led to remarkable achievements across diverse applications, from mastering Atari games through raw pixel inputs (Mnih et al., 2015), to the development of the AlphaGo system that defeated world champions in the game of Go (Silver et al., 2016), and more recently to applications in robotics (Levine et al., 2016), healthcare (Raghu et al., 2017), and autonomous vehicles (Sallab et al., 2017). Before examining how DQN agents might develop social and economic behaviors, we first establish a foundational understanding of the technical components that enable these systems to learn complex decision-making policies through experience.

The Deep Q-Network approach relies on three key technical ingredients that work in concert to enable complex behavioral learning: a nonlinear neural network architecture capable of approximating state-action value functions, a Q-function formulation that defines the reinforcement learning objective, and a backpropagation algorithm that efficiently updates network parameters based on experience. Understanding these components provides insight into how artificial agents can develop sophisticated decision-making capabilities through trial-and-error interactions with their environments. In the following sections, we examine each of these ingredients in turn, highlighting their roles in enabling DQN agents to learn not only optimal strategies for games and control tasks but potentially also social behaviors like trust and cooperation.

1.2.1 Nonlinear Neural Network Architecture

Neural networks trace their conceptual origins to the 1940s with the pioneering work of McCulloch and Pitts, who proposed a mathematical model of neural activity. The development of the perceptron by Rosenblatt in the late 1950s established an early computational model with nonlinear characteristics. However, it was not until the introduction of the backpropagation algorithm in the 1980s that multilayer neural networks with continuous nonlinear activation functions like sigmoid and hyperbolic tangent became practically trainable, allowing these networks to approximate complex functions with remarkable flexibility.

The field experienced a significant resurgence in the 2010s with the advent of deep learning, driven partly by computational advances but also by innovations in network architectures and activation functions. A particularly important development was the widespread adoption of the Rectified Linear Unit (ReLU) activation function, which offers significant computational advantages over earlier activation functions while mitigating the vanishing gradient problem that had previously hindered training of deeper networks. The ReLU function, defined simply as $f(x) = \max(0, x)$, provides a balance of nonlinearity and gradient propagation efficiency that has proven crucial for training deep networks.

While contemporary deep learning research has produced increasingly sophisticated architectures such as Convolutional Neural Networks (CNNs) for spatial data,

Recurrent Neural Networks (RNNs) for sequential data, and Transformer architectures for attention-based modeling, our work deliberately employs simpler multilayer dense (fully-connected) networks. This architectural choice is motivated by two primary considerations: interpretability and sufficiency. Dense networks with a modest number of layers provide sufficient capacity to model the decision processes relevant to social and economic games like the Trust Game, while remaining amenable to analysis of their internal representations.

As illustrated in the work of Wu et al. (2023), relatively simple feedforward networks with ReLU activation functions can successfully develop sophisticated cooperative behaviors when trained through reinforcement learning in social contexts. Their study demonstrates how DQN agents using straightforward neural architectures can exhibit trust and trustworthiness that qualitatively resemble human behavior in economic games. The architecture employed in their study consists of an input layer capturing game state information (previous actions of self and partner), followed by hidden layers using ReLU activations, and an output layer representing action values for each possible decision in the trust game.

The critical property of these networks is their universal function approximation capability—the theoretical ability to approximate any continuous function to arbitrary precision given sufficient width or depth. This property enables neural networks to capture the complex mapping from states (observations of social interactions) to values (expected future rewards from different actions) needed to develop sophisticated behavioral policies. While more complex architectures might offer advantages for certain specialized domains, the standard dense network architecture provides an ideal balance of expressive power and analytical tractability for the social and economic behaviors examined in this book.

1.2.2 Q-Learning Formulation

Reinforcement learning algorithms are fundamentally concerned with how agents should act in environments to maximize cumulative reward. The Q-learning approach, developed by Watkins in 1989 and formalized in Sutton and Barto (1998), provides a powerful framework for addressing this challenge. Q-learning is based on the concept of an action value function, denoted as $Q(s, a)$, which represents the expected cumulative future reward when taking action a in state s and following an optimal policy thereafter.

In the context of DQN agents, the Q-function is approximated by a neural network with parameters θ, written as $Q(s, a; \theta)$. The goal of training is to adjust these parameters to minimize the difference between the current Q-value estimate and the target value derived from the Bellman equation, which expresses the recursive relationship between current and future values:

$$Q^*(s, a) = \mathbb{E}[r + \gamma \max_{a'} Q^*(s', a')|s, a]$$

Here, r is the immediate reward, γ is a discount factor that determines the importance of future rewards, and s' is the next state. The Bellman equation essentially states that the value of taking action a in state s should equal the expected immediate reward plus the discounted value of the best action in the resulting state.

In the trust game context described by Wu et al. (2023), the Q-function for a trustor agent evaluates the expected future returns from sending different amounts to a trustee, taking into account both immediate payoffs and potential future reciprocation. Similarly, the Q-function for a trustee agent evaluates different return amounts, considering both immediate gains from keeping more and potential future benefits from establishing a reputation for trustworthiness. The discount factor γ plays a crucial role in this process, as it determines how much weight agents place on potential future interactions—a higher discount factor encourages more cooperative behavior through increased valuation of long-term relationships.

The Q-learning formulation, when combined with neural network function approximation, provides a formal mathematical framework for how agents can learn to balance immediate rewards against potential future benefits in social and economic interactions. This balance is precisely what enables the emergence of trust-like behaviors in artificial agents trained without explicit programming of social norms or values.

1.2.3 Backpropagation and Experience Replay

The final key ingredient in DQN systems is an efficient learning mechanism that allows neural networks to improve their Q-value approximations based on experience. Backpropagation, the cornerstone algorithm for training neural networks, enables this by computing gradients of the loss function with respect to network parameters and updating these parameters to reduce prediction errors. In DQN systems, this process is augmented with several important innovations that stabilize and enhance learning.

One critical innovation is experience replay (Mnih et al., 2015), where agents store experiences (state, action, reward, next state) in a memory buffer and randomly sample batches from this buffer for training. This approach offers several advantages: it breaks the temporal correlations in sequential data that can lead to unstable learning, it allows experiences to be used multiple times for training (improving data efficiency), and it helps prevent forgetting of rare but important experiences.

Another important technique is the use of target networks (Mnih et al., 2015), where a separate network with parameters that are periodically updated from the main network is used to generate target values for the Q-learning updates. This approach reduces the moving target problem inherent in Q-learning, where the same network is used to generate both predictions and targets, leading to potential instability.

Together, backpropagation, experience replay, and target networks form a robust learning system that allows DQN agents to gradually improve their decision-making capabilities through trial-and-error interaction with their environment. In the context of social and economic games like the trust game, these mechanisms enable agents to learn complex conditional strategies—for example, a trustor agent might learn to continue trusting only if previous trust was reciprocated, while a trustee agent might learn to balance immediate gains from exploitation against the long-term benefits of maintaining cooperative relationships.

The remarkable aspect of this learning system is that it requires no explicit programming of social norms, ethical principles, or game-theoretic equilibrium concepts. Instead, cooperative behaviors can emerge naturally from the reinforcement learning process when the environment and reward structure make cooperation beneficial in the long run. This emergent nature of social behaviors in artificial agents trained via DQN methods is precisely what makes them valuable both as practical tools for multi-agent systems and as scientific models for understanding the computational basis of social cognition.

1.2.4 Neural Networks in Practice: A Primer with Keras and TensorFlow

While the theoretical foundations of neural networks provide valuable insights into how deep learning systems operate, many readers may benefit from understanding how these concepts translate into practical implementations. This section offers a brief introduction to implementing neural networks using Keras and TensorFlow, two widely used open-source libraries that form the building blocks for more complex systems like the DQNs discussed earlier.

TensorFlow, developed by Google, serves as the underlying computational engine that efficiently handles the mathematical operations required for training neural networks. Keras, now integrated into TensorFlow, provides a high-level API that simplifies the process of building and training neural network models. Together, these tools make it possible to implement sophisticated neural networks with relatively concise code.

To illustrate how neural networks can be implemented, we present a simple example using the classic MNIST dataset (Modified National Institute of Standards and Technology database). This dataset consists of 70,000 small square 28 × 28 pixel grayscale images of handwritten single digits between 0 and 9. The task is to classify each image as the correct digit—a standard image classification problem that serves as the "Hello World" of deep learning.

The MNIST dataset is accessible through TensorFlow directly, but can also be downloaded from Kaggle (https://www.kaggle.com/datasets/oddrationale/mnist-in-csv) or viewed at the MNIST database website maintained by NYU (https://www.tensorflow.org/datasets/catalog/mnist).

This example demonstrates the basic components that would also be present in more complex applications like DQNs, including network architecture construction, compilation, and training:

```
import tensorflow as tf
from tensorflow import keras
import numpy as np

# Load the MNIST dataset
(x_train, y_train), (x_test, y_test) = keras.datasets.mnist.load_data()

# Preprocess the data
# Normalize pixel values to be between 0 and 1
x_train = x_train.astype("float32") / 255
x_test = x_test.astype("float32") / 255

# Reshape images to a flat vector
x_train = x_train.reshape(60000, 784)
x_test = x_test.reshape(10000, 784)

# Create a simple neural network model
def create_simple_model():
    """
    Creates a simple feedforward neural network using Keras.

    Returns:
    keras.Model: Compiled neural network model
    """
    # Create a sequential model
    model = keras.Sequential([
        # Input layer with flatten operation
        keras.layers.InputLayer(input_shape=(784,)),

        # Hidden layers with ReLU activation functions
        keras.layers.Dense(128, activation='relu'),
        keras.layers.Dense(64, activation='relu'),

        # Output layer with softmax activation for classification
        keras.layers.Dense(10, activation='softmax')
    ])

    # Compile the model with categorical crossentropy loss and Adam optimizer
    model.compile(
        optimizer='adam',
        loss='sparse_categorical_crossentropy',
        metrics=['accuracy']
    )

    return model

# Create and train the model
model = create_simple_model()

# Print the model summary
model.summary()

# Train the model
model.fit(
    x_train, y_train,
    batch_size=128,
    epochs=5,
```

```
    validation_split=0.1
)

# Evaluate the model on test data
test_loss, test_acc = model.evaluate(x_test, y_test)
print(f"Test accuracy: {test_acc:.4f}")
```

This example demonstrates several key concepts in neural network implementation:

- **Data preparation**: Loading and preprocessing the input data
- **Model architecture**: Defining the structure of the neural network with input, hidden, and output layers
- **Activation functions**: Using ReLU for hidden layers and softmax for the output classification layer
- **Model compilation**: Configuring the learning process with an optimizer and loss function
- **Training**: Fitting the model to the data with specified batch size and number of epochs
- **Evaluation**: Testing the model's performance on unseen data

The dense layers with ReLU activations in this example are similar to those used in the DQN architectures discussed earlier in this chapter. In a DQN implementation, the primary differences would be in the network's output (representing Q-values for actions rather than classification probabilities) and the training process (using experience replay and target networks rather than supervised learning).

Readers interested in exploring neural networks further can take advantage of several excellent resources:

- TensorFlow's official tutorials: https://www.tensorflow.org/tutorials
- Keras documentation: https://keras.io/getting_started/
- TensorFlow's comprehensive MNIST tutorial with detailed explanations: https://www.tensorflow.org/tutorials/keras/classification
- Stanford CS231n's explanation of Convolutional Neural Networks with MNIST examples: https://cs231n.github.io/
- TensorFlow Playground for visual experimentation: https://playground.tensorflow.org/
- Google Colab notebooks for running examples without local setup: https://colab.research.google.com/
- A complete MNIST example notebook: https://colab.research.google.com/github/tensorflow/docs/blob/master/site/en/tutorials/quickstart/beginner.ipynb
- Deep Learning for Computer Vision blog with MNIST walkthrough: https://machinelearningmastery.com/how-to-develop-a-convolutional-neural-network-from-scratch-for-mnist-handwritten-digit-classification/

For those wishing to progress from this basic example to reinforcement learning implementations like DQNs, TensorFlow's reinforcement learning library (TF-Agents) provides tools and tutorials: https://www.tensorflow.org/agents

Understanding the basics of neural network implementation provides a foundation for appreciating the more complex systems discussed throughout this book. While the social and economic behaviors emerging from AI systems require sophisticated architectures and training protocols, they are built upon these fundamental components of modern deep learning.

1.3 The GPT-Language-based Experimental Economics System (GLEES)

1.3.1 Conceptual Overview of GLEES

The GPT-Language-based Experimental Economics System (GLEES) (Chen & Wu, 2025) emerged as a methodological approach to address fundamental questions at the intersection of Large Language Models (LLMs) and experimental economics. As LLMs like GPT-4, Claude, and others increasingly enter decision-making domains previously reserved for humans, understanding their social and economic behaviors has become not merely an academic curiosity but a practical necessity. GLEES was developed specifically to systematically investigate how LLM-based agents might interact, make decisions, and potentially develop cooperative or competitive strategies in controlled economic environments.

The conceptual foundation of GLEES rests on several key observations about the unique characteristics of LLMs. First, while reinforcement learning approaches like DQNs can develop emergent cooperative behaviors through extensive trial-and-error interactions, LLMs present a fundamentally different paradigm—one where behaviors appear to be inherited from training data rather than learned through direct experience. This distinction raises profound questions about the nature of social intelligence in LLMs and whether these systems can exhibit consistent economic behaviors across varied contexts without explicit reinforcement learning.

Second, as LLMs become increasingly deployed in real-world economic decision-making contexts—from automated trading systems to customer service interactions—understanding their behavioral patterns takes on practical significance. Without a systematic framework for studying these behaviors, we risk deploying LLM-based systems with unpredictable social and economic tendencies. GLEES addresses this gap by providing a controlled experimental environment where LLM behaviors can be systematically cataloged and analyzed.

The design of GLEES was driven by three primary objectives that distinguish it from previous approaches to studying LLM behavior. First, the system needed to create and maintain a population of LLM-based agents that function independently of the specific games they play—mirroring how human experimental subjects bring consistent personalities and preferences across experimental tasks. This agent independence enables researchers to study behavioral consistency and detect meaningful patterns that transcend specific game structures.

Second, GLEES was designed with game flexibility as a core principle, allowing for the implementation of any economic game without requiring extensive reconfiguration of the underlying system. This flexibility enables systematic comparison across different economic scenarios, from simple trust games to complex market institutions, using the same population of LLM-based agents. Such comparability is essential for building a comprehensive understanding of LLM economic behavior.

Finally, GLEES was constructed to be model-agnostic, functioning independently of the specific LLM being used. This design choice facilitates comparative studies across different LLM models and versions, providing insights into how model architecture and training methodologies influence economic and social behaviors. As the field of language models continues to evolve rapidly, this agnosticism ensures that GLEES remains relevant across successive generations of LLMs.

Beyond these technical considerations, GLEES addresses a more fundamental methodological question: how can we meaningfully study decision-making entities that differ fundamentally from humans in their cognitive architecture? Unlike human experimental subjects who bring lifelong experiences and intrinsic motivations to economic games, LLMs have neither intrinsic utilities nor personal histories outside the experimental context. GLEES addresses this challenge through prompt engineering that creates persistent agent identities with consistent personalities and memories across interactions.

This approach represents a departure from traditional experimental economics with human subjects, where personality differences are typically treated as random variation rather than experimental variables. With GLEES, researchers can systematically vary LLM agent characteristics and study how these variations influence economic decisions—opening new avenues for understanding the relationship between personality traits and economic behavior that would be difficult to study with human subjects.

In essence, GLEES serves as a methodological bridge between traditional experimental economics and LLM research, enabling controlled investigations of how language model-based agents interact, make decisions, and potentially develop cooperative or competitive strategies across repeated interactions. By providing a standardized framework for studying LLM economic behavior, GLEES contributes to our understanding of both the capabilities of current language models and the broader implications of deploying these systems in economic contexts.

1.3.2 A Component-Based Design of LLM Agents

To study the social and economic behaviors of Large Language Models in controlled experimental settings, we need agents that can participate in economic games with consistent identities, stable preferences, and the ability to learn from past interactions—just as human subjects do. Traditional LLMs, while capable of sophisticated reasoning, lack persistent identities and memories across separate interactions. Hence, we design an LLM agent framework with three essential components: a Cognitive Interface that provides reasoning capabilities, a Persona that establishes consistent preferences, and Episodic Memory that maintains a record of past experiences.

Cognitive Interface—This component connects the agent to an external LLM (such as GPT-4 or Claude) that provides general reasoning capabilities, domain knowledge, and language understanding. The Cognitive Interface serves as the agent's link to sophisticated cognitive processing without requiring us to build these capabilities from scratch. By leveraging pre-trained LLMs, agents gain access to rich knowledge about economic concepts, social norms, and decision-making strategies that would be prohibitively expensive to develop independently. This separation of general reasoning from agent-specific traits also enables researchers to maintain experimental control while studying how different agents respond to identical scenarios.

Persona—This component establishes the agent's persistent identity and preference structure, including characteristics such as risk tolerance, fairness orientation, professional background, and decision-making style. The Persona ensures that agents maintain consistent behavior patterns across multiple interactions, mirroring how human subjects bring stable personalities to experimental settings. Without this component, LLM responses would lack the consistency required for meaningful economic experiments. By systematically varying persona characteristics, researchers can create heterogeneous populations of agents and study how specific traits influence economic decisions—an approach that offers new possibilities for understanding the relationship between personality and economic behavior.

Episodic Memory—This component maintains a record of the agent's specific experiences and interactions within the experimental environment. Unlike the general knowledge provided by the Cognitive Interface, Episodic Memory contains personal history unique to each individual agent—what it has done, observed, earned, and learned from previous interactions. This memory is essential for studying economic phenomena that involve repeated interactions, such as trust-building, reciprocity, and learning from experience. Without Episodic Memory, agents could not maintain consistent relationships with other agents or adapt their strategies based on past outcomes. This component enables researchers to analyze how behavior evolves over time and how past experiences shape current economic decisions.

The implementation of LLM-based agents in GLEES (Chen & Wu, 2025) reflects this component-based design while adapting it to practical experimental requirements. GLEES constructs prompts with distinct sections that align with our theoretical framework: the "Persona" section establishes consistent agent identity across interactions, directly corresponding to our Persona component; "History" statements maintain agent-specific experiences across decision rounds, implementing the Episodic Memory component; while the underlying LLM API serves as the Cognitive Interface. Importantly, the "Game Instructions" section in GLEES is conceptually distinct from these agent components—rather than being intrinsic to the agent, it represents the experimental environment in which the agent operates, similar to how written instructions in traditional economics experiments provide context to human participants without altering their fundamental characteristics. This clean separation between agent attributes and experimental conditions allows researchers to systematically study how consistent agent identities respond to varying economic scenarios. We will discuss the economics experiment design and related prompt engineering in greater detail later in this chapter, focusing on how these elements create controlled environments for studying LLM social behaviors.

GLEES maintains a population of distinct LLM-based agents, each possessing its own independent persona and episodic memory that persist across multiple interactions. While these persona and memory components remain agent specific, the cognitive interface typically connects to a single underlying language model through API calls, though the system's architecture provides flexibility to connect different agents to different LLM implementations if desired. Importantly, each API call to the language model is stateless and independent, with no information persisting between calls except what is explicitly included in the prompts. Consequently, the permanence and continuity of an agent's identity rely solely on its persona and accumulated memory components, which are systematically incorporated into each prompt when the agent is called to act. This design ensures that agents maintain consistent identities and decision patterns while enabling researchers to study how these patterns evolve through experience. We will discuss how prompts are engineered in greater detail later in this chapter.

1.3.3 Economics Experiment Implementation

To systematically investigate the social and economic behaviors of LLM-based agents, GLEES requires a flexible yet structured approach to implementing experimental scenarios. The system's design emphasizes modularity, reusability, and separation of concerns—allowing researchers to focus on experimental design rather than technical implementation details. The economics experiment implementation within GLEES consists of several key components that work together to create controlled interactive environments.

Game Definition—At the core of GLEES is a game definition architecture implemented as a data structure with associated functions that execute the logic of various economic experiments. This approach abstracts the mechanics of each game into a standardized format that the system can process independently of the specific agents participating. By encoding games as structured data rather than hard-coded procedures, GLEES achieves flexibility—enabling researchers to implement virtually any economic scenario from simple trust games to complex market institutions without altering the underlying system architecture. This design choice facilitates comparative studies across different economic paradigms while maintaining methodological consistency, as the same population of agents can participate in diverse experimental scenarios without requiring reconfiguration of the system itself.

Player Role Abstraction—A critical design element in GLEES is the clear separation between player roles and the specific agents who fulfill those roles. The system defines player roles (such as "proposer" or "responder" in an ultimatum game) as abstract entities with specific functions and responsibilities within the game structure. During execution, these abstract roles are assigned to specific AI agents from the available population. This abstraction creates a clean interface between the game mechanics and agent characteristics, enabling flexible matching protocols and ensuring that experimental designs remain independent of the specific agents participating. From a coding perspective, this separation simplifies game implementation as developers can focus on the logic associated with each role without concern for which agent will ultimately play that role—mirroring how experimental economists design protocols without knowing which specific human subjects will participate.

Stage-based Interaction Progression—GLEES organizes experimental interactions into discrete stages that represent natural units of decision-making and information exchange. Each stage definition contains a list of players who take action, functions to generate appropriate prompts for soliciting those actions, and functions to process responses and advance the game state accordingly. This stage-based architecture provides several advantages: it breaks complex interactions into manageable components, enables precise control over information flow, and creates natural synchronization points in multi-agent interactions. From an implementation standpoint, stages serve as the primary unit of both timing and functional organization—allowing for sophisticated experiment designs that combine synchronous and asynchronous interactions within a single experimental protocol. The specific prompt elements needed for each stage (such as decision options or relevant contextual information) are stored in data structures that are included directly in the stage definition, though we will discuss prompt engineering in greater detail later.

Data Tracking—Experimental economics requires systematic data collection to draw meaningful conclusions about behavior. GLEES implements comprehensive data tracking through variables defined within each game structure that record every significant interaction, decision, and outcome throughout the experimental session. This approach ensures that researchers have access to complete experimental records for analysis without requiring additional instrumentation. The system automatically maintains these variables across multiple rounds of interaction, creating rich longitudinal datasets that can reveal patterns in how agent behavior evolves over time. From a coding perspective, this integrated data collection simplifies experimental procedures by eliminating the need for separate data recording mechanisms and ensuring consistent measurement across all interactions within an experimental session.

The original implementation of GLEES was developed in R, leveraging its statistical capabilities and data handling features. The system has also been translated into Python and used in a project, taking advantage of Python's extensive machine learning and natural language processing libraries. Interestingly, initial experimentation has shown that advanced LLMs can understand and use the system by generating appropriate game definitions and related code when prompted with the system's requirements. One successful experiment demonstrated this capability, suggesting potential pathways for reducing implementation barriers for researchers without extensive programming expertise.

1.3.4 Prompt Engineering and Execution Flow in GLEES

We have touched on aspects of prompt engineering in previous sections when discussing both LLM-based agents and the economics experiment implementation. However, since prompts are drawn from multiple components of the system and constitute the central mechanism for controlling LLM behavior, it is useful to consolidate this information in one place. As highlighted earlier, each prompt is constructed dynamically from different sources within the GLEES architecture, creating a comprehensive set of instructions that guide the LLM's responses in specific experimental contexts.

Prompt Components and Sources—The GLEES system constructs prompts from four primary components, each drawn from different parts of the system architecture. The "Persona" component establishes agent identity and is stored as part of the individual AI agent's attributes, independent of any specific game. In implementations using ChatGPT, this component is fed into the "system" part of the API input. The "Game Instructions" component provides general information about the experimental scenario and remains consistent across roles and game states; these instructions are stored in the game definition. The "History" component contains a sequence of statements about an agent's past experiences, generated by calling a history function after each period and stored in the agent's memory. Finally, the "Stage Instructions" component provides specific directions for the current interaction and includes dynamic information from the game state; these are generated from the stage definition in the game structure. The latter three components are typically combined into the "user" part of the API input.

Prompt Assembly Process—When an AI agent needs to act, the system dynamically assembles these components into a coherent prompt. This assembly process follows a specific sequence designed to provide the LLM with appropriate context while maintaining the agent's consistent identity. The persona is always included to ensure behavioral consistency across interactions. Game instructions provide the general framework for decision-making. History statements can be included based on researcher preferences—all periods, only the most recent N periods, or none at all—enabling controlled experiments on the effects of memory on economic behavior. Stage instructions typically appear at the end of the prompt, providing the specific decision context and action requirements for the current interaction. This structured approach to prompt construction ensures that agents maintain consistent identities while responding appropriately to their current experimental context.

The prompt engineering approach in GLEES represents an adaptation of general LLM prompting techniques to the specific requirements of economic experiments. By systematically constructing prompts from well-defined components stored in different parts of the system architecture, GLEES creates a controlled experimental environment where LLM-based agents can exhibit consistent economic behaviors while maintaining their unique characteristics across multiple interactions.

Execution Flow—The operational flow of GLEES follows a structured sequence that brings together the previously discussed components. The process begins with creating a population of LLM agents, each with its own persona and initially empty memory store. The system then implements a matching protocol that assigns these agents to specific roles within the game structure based on the experimental design—this might involve fixed pairings, random matching, or other protocols depending on research objectives. Once assignments are complete, the system initializes the game state and begins execution. At each stage of the game, the system identifies which agents need to act based on the stage definition and matching protocol. For each active agent, the system constructs a prompt by assembling the agent's persona, relevant game instructions, appropriate history elements, and specific stage instructions as previously described. This prompt is then sent via API call to the underlying LLM, which generates a response representing the agent's action. After all required agents have acted, the system invokes the game logic code defined for that stage, which processes the agents' responses and updates the game state accordingly. This sequence repeats across all defined stages and periods of the experiment, with the system maintaining consistent agent identities throughout while updating their memories with new experiences from each interaction.

1.4 Behavioral Economics Frameworks Applied to AI Systems

To effectively analyze the social and economic behaviors of AI systems, we must establish appropriate methodological frameworks that bridge traditional behavioral economics with the unique challenges of studying artificial agents. While DQNs and LLMs differ fundamentally in their architecture and learning mechanisms, both can be examined through established behavioral economics paradigms that address key dimensions such as social preferences and individual risk attitudes. This section outlines key methodological approaches that enable rigorous investigation of AI economic decision-making and social behaviors, providing the analytical foundation for the research presented in subsequent chapters.

1.4.1 Methodological Framework

Economics experiments provide controlled environments to measure specific behaviors and preferences while isolating key variables of interest. Originally developed to study human decision-making, these experimental paradigms can be adapted to investigate AI social behaviors. As established in the methodological frameworks of experimental economics (Plott & Smith, 2008; Smith, 1982), standard games such as the trust game, ultimatum game, prisoner's dilemma, and public goods game offer structured scenarios to evaluate cooperation, fairness, trust, and strategic reasoning in artificial agents. For DQN-based systems, these games can be implemented as reinforcement learning environments where agents learn through repeated interactions. For LLM-based agents in GLEES, these games can be presented through carefully structured prompts that describe the decision context and available choices. The consistent application of these experimental paradigms across different AI architectures enables systematic comparison of emergent behaviors and learning patterns.

Revealed preference analysis focuses on inferring underlying preferences or utilities from observed choices rather than self-reported attitudes. This approach is particularly valuable for studying AI systems, which cannot introspect or self-report on their "mental states" in the way human subjects can. By observing how AI agents make trade-offs across different decision scenarios, researchers can identify patterns in their apparent preferences and decision rules. This analysis enables precise comparisons between different AI systems and human behavior patterns, helping to characterize the decision-making approaches that emerge in artificial agents when faced with social and economic choices.

Comparative benchmarking involves systematically comparing AI behavior against relevant reference points—most commonly human behavior in identical decision environments. This methodological approach is essential for determining whether AI social behaviors are truly similar to human patterns or merely superficially resemblant. Several types of benchmarks are particularly valuable when studying AI social behavior, including human performance in identical experimental tasks, theoretical predictions from game theory, cross-system comparisons between different AI architectures, and longitudinal benchmarks tracking how AI behavior evolves across repeated interactions. By establishing these comparative frameworks, researchers can move beyond simple anthropomorphization of AI behavior to develop nuanced understandings of where, how, and why artificial systems exhibit social and economic behaviors that resemble—or differ from—human patterns.

1.4.2 Behavioral Dimensions of Economic Choices

Behavioral economics provides several well-established dimensions for analyzing decision-making, enabling researchers to characterize behaviors across different populations—including artificial agents. Drawing from comprehensive treatments by Camerer (2011) and Kagel and Roth (1995), we identify four primary dimensions that are particularly relevant when studying AI social and economic behavior:

Risk and Uncertainty Attitudes—How agents respond to probabilistic outcomes and uncertain environments reveals fundamental aspects of their decision processes. Risk attitudes are typically measured through lottery choices and other controlled gambles, revealing whether an agent is risk-averse (preferring guaranteed outcomes over risky prospects with equal expected value), risk-neutral (choosing based solely on expected value), or risk-seeking (preferring risky prospects) (Holt & Laury, 2002; Kahneman & Tversky, 1979). Beyond simple risk attitudes, behavioral economics examines probability weighting—how agents subjectively evaluate probabilistic events—and ambiguity aversion, which describes responses to unknown probability distributions. These dimensions are particularly important when evaluating AI decision-making in uncertain environments, where probability estimation and risk management are essential components of effective behavior.

Social Preferences—Traditional economic models assume self-interested utility maximization, but decades of behavioral research have documented how human decision-makers incorporate others' outcomes into their utilities. Social preferences characterize behavior along dimensions including fairness considerations (whether agents prefer equitable distributions), reciprocity (conditional cooperation based on others' actions), trust and trustworthiness (willingness to accept vulnerability and honor trust), and altruism/spite (unconditional positive or negative regard for others' outcomes) (Charness & Rabin, 2002; Fehr & Schmidt, 1999). Games like the Ultimatum Game, Trust Game, and Public Goods Game provide standardized environments to measure these preferences. As AI systems increasingly participate in multi-agent environments, understanding their emergent social preferences becomes critical for predicting interaction patterns, particularly as these preferences may differ significantly from those programmed or reinforced during training.

Bounded Rationality and Biases—Perfectly rational decision-making requires unlimited computational capacity and strict adherence to probability theory and utility maximization—conditions that human decision-makers systematically violate. Bounded rationality (Simon, 1955) characterizes these deviations, starting with quantal response models (McKelvey & Palfrey, 1995) that describe probabilistic choice with systematic errors. Other important aspects include framing effects (sensitivity to how options are presented), anchoring (undue influence of initially presented values), loss aversion (asymmetric valuation of gains versus losses), and limitations in computational capacity. As AI systems become more complex, they may develop their own forms of bounded rationality—not from cognitive limitations per se, but from approximations necessitated by their architecture, training data, or optimization processes.

Learning—How agents adapt their behavior through experience represents a crucial dimension of decision-making. Learning examines adaptation across repeated interactions, including reinforcement learning (adjusting behavior based on experienced outcomes), belief-based learning (updating mental models of the environment or other agents), experience-weighted attraction (integrating both mechanisms), and the development of strategic sophistication over time (Camerer & Ho, 1999; Erev & Roth, 1998). For AI systems, learning mechanisms are especially important as they represent the primary pathway through which behaviors develop and adapt. DQNs explicitly implement reinforcement learning algorithms, while LLMs appear to demonstrate forms of in-context learning despite not being explicitly trained to do so.

These four dimensions provide complementary perspectives on agent behavior, offering a comprehensive toolkit for characterizing the social and economic behaviors of both humans and artificial systems. Importantly, these behaviors do not exist in isolation but are modulated by contextual and environmental factors. Cultural influences, institutional structures, information availability, and social context can all significantly modify expressions of risk attitudes, social preferences, bounded rationality, and learning processes. In AI systems, these contextual factors may manifest through training data composition, deployment environment characteristics, or system prompting. Throughout this book, we apply these behavioral dimensions to analyze AI decision-making, identifying both parallels to human behavior and unique patterns specific to different AI architectures.

1.5 Beyond Human Behavioral Frameworks: AI-Specific Research Challenges

While behavioral economics provides valuable frameworks for analyzing decision-making, the study of AI social and economic behaviors introduces distinct research challenges that extend beyond traditional approaches. Behavioral economics was developed to understand human decision-making processes, with experimental methods and analytical frameworks tailored to human subjects. However, as AI systems increasingly participate in economic and social contexts, we must develop new methodological approaches specifically designed for understanding artificial agents. This section examines two fundamental research challenges that emerge when studying AI behavior: the emergence of complex behaviors beyond simple objective functions and the unique opportunity to systematically control behavioral characteristics.

1.5.1 Emergent Behaviors Beyond Objective Functions

A striking feature of modern AI systems is their tendency to exhibit complex behaviors that appear to transcend the simple objectives encoded in their training processes. In DQN systems, the formal objective is straightforward: maximize the expected discounted future reward as expressed in the Bellman equation. Yet, as demonstrated by Wu et al. (2023) and further examined in Chap. 2, these systems can develop social behaviors resembling trust and reciprocity—sophisticated strategies that were neither explicitly programmed nor directly rewarded during training. Similarly, LLMs are fundamentally trained on next-token prediction, a purely statistical task with no inherent social component. Nevertheless, these systems demonstrate complex social reasoning, normative judgments, and strategic thinking in economic games, as shown in the GLEES experiments discussed in Chap. 3.

This gap between an AI system's formal objective function and its observed behaviors raises important questions about the mechanisms through which complex social behaviors emerge. For DQNs, one hypothesis is that social behaviors represent optimal solutions to the multi-agent reinforcement learning problem—cooperative strategies simply maximize long-term rewards more effectively than non-cooperative ones in certain environments. For LLMs, social behaviors likely reflect patterns present in training data, where human-written text encodes social norms, strategic thinking, and cooperative behaviors. Understanding these emergence mechanisms is crucial for developing AI systems with predictable and beneficial social behaviors.

One promising approach to understanding these emergent social behaviors involves directly analyzing the internal representations within neural networks. By examining activation patterns, gradient flows, and learned value functions, researchers can investigate how social and behavioral information is encoded and stored within the network architecture. This approach goes beyond treating neural networks as black boxes and instead seeks to understand the computational mechanisms that give rise to sophisticated social behaviors. Chapter 2 explores this analytical approach in detail, showing how internal network representations can reveal insights into both how artificial agents develop social intelligence and potentially how similar mechanisms might operate in biological neural systems. While the analysis in Chap. 2 focuses on social learning contexts, the interpretability techniques themselves represent general approaches applicable across neural network architectures and problem domains.

The emergence of cooperation in multi-agent AI environments presents both methodological challenges and research opportunities. When multiple AI systems interact repeatedly, they may naturally evolve toward cooperative equilibria—not because cooperation was programmed as an objective, but because it emerges as a stable strategy. This raises methodological concerns about circularity in AI evaluation, particularly when AI systems are trained or evaluated against other AI systems. If an AI system develops cooperative tendencies that are then used to evaluate other AI systems, we risk creating artificial behavioral benchmarks that have little relevance to real-world deployment contexts where systems will interact with humans or differently-trained AI.

However, this potential circularity also presents a valuable opportunity to study how emergent dynamics develop in multi-agent AI environments. By controlling initial conditions, interaction structures, and learning mechanisms, researchers can systematically investigate how and when cooperation emerges, whether it remains stable across environmental perturbations, and which architectural features promote or inhibit cooperative equilibria. These insights can inform the design of AI systems intended for deployment in multi-agent settings, from financial markets to supply chain optimization. Understanding emergent social dynamics in controlled AI environments may also provide broader insights into the foundations of cooperative behavior, though caution must be exercised when extrapolating from artificial to biological systems.

1.5.2 Persona Control and Behavioral Variation

A second distinctive feature of AI behavioral research is the expanded ability to control inputs that influence behavioral outcomes. While human subjects in economic experiments can be influenced through framing, incentives, and experimental manipulations, they still bring underlying traits, preferences, and experiences that are difficult to isolate or precisely control. Experimenters can certainly affect human behavior, but disentangling the influence of pre-existing individual differences remains challenging. AI systems, in contrast, allow researchers to systematically vary specific inputs—such as discount factors in DQNs or persona descriptions in LLMs—and observe how these variations affect emergent behaviors, even though the relationship between these inputs and resulting behaviors remains complex.

In DQN systems, parameters such as discount factors, network architectures, and reward structures can be systematically varied, enabling researchers to directly investigate how specific architectural choices influence emergent social behaviors. As shown in studies of the trust game (Wu et al., 2023), manipulating a DQN agent's discount factor—its valuation of future rewards—can significantly alter cooperative tendencies, with higher discount factors generally promoting more trustworthy behavior. Similarly, the presence or absence of memory mechanisms critically determines whether agents develop trust-like behaviors.

LLM-based agents present even more extensive possibilities for controlled behavioral variation through prompt engineering. The GLEES framework enables the creation of AI agents with specific behavioral profiles—risk-averse or risk-seeking, cooperation-oriented or competition-oriented, fairness-prioritizing or outcome-maximizing. These "personas" can be systematically varied while maintaining other agent characteristics constant, allowing for clean experimental designs that isolate the effects of specific behavioral traits on economic decisions. As demonstrated in the ultimatum game experiments discussed in Chap. 3, LLM-based agents can maintain consistent behavioral profiles across multiple interactions and adapt these profiles based on experience.

This capacity for systematic input variation enables distinct research approaches focused specifically on understanding AI behavior. Researchers can create populations of AI agents with systematically varied parameters, allowing for controlled investigation of how specific inputs influence economic and social behaviors in artificial systems. For example, market simulations can be conducted with systematic variations in risk preferences, time horizons, or social preferences to understand how these characteristics influence price dynamics and equilibrium outcomes. Such systematic variation allows for more precise identification of causal relationships between behavioral traits and economic outcomes than is possible in human studies, where traits cannot be experimentally manipulated.

It is important to emphasize that the goal of such research is not to use AI as a proxy for understanding human behavior, but rather to understand AI behavior as a distinct phenomenon with increasing real-world importance. As AI systems take on greater roles in economic decision-making—from algorithmic trading to resource allocation—understanding their behavioral characteristics becomes essential for predicting and managing their impacts on economic systems.

1.5.3 Methodological Implications

These distinctive aspects of AI behavioral research necessitate adaptations to traditional experimental economics methodologies. First, standard economic games must be modified to accommodate the different interfaces through which AI systems receive information and express decisions. For DQNs, games must be formalized as reinforcement learning environments with appropriate state, action, and reward structures. For LLMs, games must be expressed through carefully designed prompts that provide all necessary context and instructions.

Second, appropriate benchmarks must be established for evaluating AI behavior. While human behavior provides one relevant reference point, the differences in learning mechanisms between humans and AI systems suggest that additional benchmarks may be needed. These might include theoretical optimal strategies, comparison across different AI architectures, or longitudinal evaluation of behavioral stability and adaptation.

Third, experimental designs must account for the unique capabilities and limitations of AI systems. For example, while LLMs can process and generate natural language, they lack intrinsic motivation and may be sensitive to subtle variations in how instructions are framed. Similarly, while DQNs can learn through extensive trial-and-error that would exhaust human subjects, they may be limited in their ability to generalize learned behaviors to novel contexts.

Finally, researchers must develop appropriate interpretive frameworks for AI behavior. Traditional behavioral economics often interprets observed behaviors in terms of underlying preferences, beliefs, and motivations. However, AI systems may exhibit behaviors that superficially resemble human patterns without sharing the underlying mechanisms. Careful analysis is needed to distinguish behaviors that reflect similar computational principles from those that merely mimic human patterns through different processes.

As the field of AI behavioral economics develops, these methodological challenges will likely require interdisciplinary collaboration between economists, computer scientists, psychologists, and ethicists. By developing robust methodologies specifically designed for studying AI behavior, researchers can establish a foundation for understanding how these increasingly important systems will function in economic and social contexts.

The research directions outlined in this chapter only scratch the surface of the emerging field at the intersection of artificial intelligence, behavioral economics, and social psychology. This book focuses on providing evidence and analysis for select advances in understanding AI social and economic behaviors, particularly those related to trust, cooperation, and strategic decision-making. While we examine specific mechanisms through which these behaviors emerge in both DQN and LLM systems, many questions remain unexplored. As AI systems increasingly participate in economic and social contexts, developing appropriate frameworks for understanding their behavior becomes not merely an academic exercise but a practical necessity. Our goal is not to provide a comprehensive treatment of all potential approaches, but rather to contribute to the ongoing dialogue and offer analytical perspectives that may prove useful for future research in this rapidly evolving domain.

1.5.4 *Tacit Knowledge and Ecological Validity in AI Behavioral Research*

Understanding the behavioral patterns of AI agents requires careful consideration of what knowledge these systems possess and how it generalizes beyond experimental settings. Recent theoretical work on Polanyi's concept of tacit knowledge in AI systems (Bizzarri et al., 2022) provides a framework for interpreting our findings, while research on ecological validity highlights limitations of controlled experimental approaches.

Tacit Knowledge in Artificial Agents

Polanyi's (1966) observation that "we know more than we can tell" captures the essence of tacit knowledge: implicit understanding that guides behavior without explicit representation or conscious articulation. Our experimental findings demonstrate that AI agents develop functional tacit knowledge through both emergent learning and inherited patterns.

For DQN-based agents (Chap. 2), trust and cooperation strategies emerge without explicit programming of social norms. Neural network analysis (Sect. 2.6) reveals how social information becomes encoded in implicit representations, with agents developing trigger strategies and reputation-based decision rules that were never directly taught. The network "knows" when to trust through distributed patterns of connection weights rather than explicit rules. This represents a manifestation of functional tacit knowledge.

For LLM-based agents (Chap. 3), persona engineering effects demonstrate the activation of tacit social norms inherited from training data. When prompted with behavioral characteristics, these agents systematically exhibit corresponding decision patterns across multiple domains including risk preferences, fairness judgments, and strategic behaviors. This suggests they have absorbed implicit behavioral knowledge from human-generated text. The effectiveness of persona manipulation indicates that LLMs possess tacit understanding of how behavioral traits manifest across different contexts.

These findings show that AI systems can develop and utilize functional tacit knowledge. Implicit behavioral patterns guide decisions without explicit representation. This represents a capability for artificial agents operating in social and economic environments.

Ecological Validity and Contextual Generalization

Controlled experimental settings necessarily abstract away from the contextual fabric of real-world environments. Research in clinical AI illustrates this challenge: identical patient data can have different predictive meaning depending on the context in which it was collected. Routine checkups versus emergency visits yield different outcome predictions for the same numerical values (Beaulieu-Jones et al., 2021). Our experimental paradigms (trust games, ultimatum games, risk preference elicitation tasks) similarly strip away contextual complexity to achieve experimental control. Real-world trust, cooperation, and risk-taking occur within contexts including legal frameworks, cultural norms, reputational systems, power dynamics, and economic conditions that our experiments necessarily simplify. This raises the question of ecological validity: whether behaviors learned or measured in experimental settings generalize to deployment environments.

We have taken steps to address this concern through cross-task validation. Chapter 4 demonstrates that behavioral traits measured in one experimental context (staircase risk preference task) successfully predict behavior in alternative contexts (investment allocation decisions and insurance purchase tasks), achieving Kendall's tau correlations ranging from 0.53 to 0.74. This provides evidence for behavioral consistency across related decision contexts within the risk preference domain, suggesting that measured traits capture stable characteristics rather than task-specific responses.

However, these validation efforts remain within experimental settings in the same behavioral domain. The tasks vary in their specific structure and framing, but all involve controlled presentation of options with clear probabilistic or financial parameters. Whether AI behavioral patterns generalize to fully naturalistic deployment environments (where contextual factors are implicit, stakes are ambiguous, and social dynamics are complex) represents a direction for future research.

Implications for Interpretation and Deployment

This analysis yields several implications. First, AI agents demonstrably develop functional tacit knowledge within experimental domains. This represents a genuine capability rather than a limitation. The ability to learn implicit behavioral patterns without explicit programming enables flexible adaptation to social and economic environments.

Second, the ecological validity of experimental findings for real-world deployment remains an open empirical question. Performance in controlled settings provides evidence of capability but does not guarantee equivalent performance in contextually richer environments. Deployment of AI agents in social or economic contexts requires careful validation in target environments, with attention to contextual factors that may influence behavioral appropriateness.

Third, the distinction between functional tacit knowledge (what AI agents demonstrably possess) and ecological contextual knowledge (what may be required for robust deployment) suggests directions for future research. Developing methods for AI systems to acquire, represent, and utilize contextual knowledge represents a challenge for the field. Alternatively, developing methods for AI systems to recognize when learned patterns may not apply in novel contexts also represents an avenue for investigation.

References

Akata, E., Schulz, L., Coda-Forno, J., Oh, S. J., Bethge, M., & Schulz, E. (2025). *Playing repeated games with large language models*. Advances in Neural Information Processing Systems, 37.

Beaulieu-Jones, B. K., Yuan, W. Brat, G. A., Beam, A. L., Weber, G., Ruffin, M., & Kohane, I. S. (2021). Machine learning for patient risk stratification: Standing on, or looking over, the shoulders of clinicians? *npj Digital Medicine, 4*(1), 62. https://doi.org/10.1038/s41746-021-00426-3

Bizzarri, F., Giuliani, A., & Mocenni, C. (2022). Awareness: An empirical model. *Frontiers in Psychology, 13*, Article 933183. https://doi.org/10.3389/fpsyg.2022.933183

Brewer, P., Juybari, J., & Moberly, R. (2024). A comparison of zero- and minimal-intelligence agendas in majority-rule voting models. *Journal of Economic Interaction and Coordination, 19*, 403–437. https://doi.org/10.1007/s11403-023-00387-8

Camerer, C. F. (2011). *Behavioral game theory: Experiments in strategic interaction*. Princeton University Press.

Camerer, C., & Ho, T.-H. (1999). Experience-weighted attraction learning in normal form games. *Econometrica, 67*(4), 827–874.

Charness, G., & Rabin, M. (2002). Understanding social preferences with simple tests. *The Quarterly Journal of Economics, 117*(3), 817–869.

Chen, K.-Y., & Wu, D. (2025). *GPT-Language-based Experimental Economics System (GLEES)* (Working Paper).

Chen, Y., Kirshner, S. N., Ovchinnikov, A., Andiappan, M., & Jenkin, T. (2025). A manager and an AI walk into a bar: Does ChatGPT make biased decisions like we do? *Manufacturing & Service Operations Management, 27*(2), 354–368. https://doi.org/10.1287/msom.2023.0279

Dafoe, A., Hughes, E., Bachrach, Y., Collins, T., McKee, K. R., Leibo, J. Z., Larson, K., & Graepel, T. (2021). Cooperative AI: Machines must learn to find common ground. *Nature, 593*(7857), 33–36. https://doi.org/10.1038/d41586-021-01170-0

Erev, I., & Roth, A. E. (1998). Predicting how people play games: Reinforcement learning in experimental games with unique, mixed strategy equilibria. *American Economic Review, 88*(4), 848–881.

Fehr, E., & Schmidt, K. M. (1999). A theory of fairness, competition, and cooperation. *The Quarterly Journal of Economics, 114*(3), 817–868.

Goli, A., & Singh, A. (2024). Frontiers: Can large language models capture human preferences? *Marketing Science, 43*(4), 709–722. https://doi.org/10.1287/mksc.2024.0017

Holt, C. A., & Laury, S. K. (2002). Risk aversion and incentive effects. *American Economic Review, 92*(5), 1644–1655.

Kagel, J. H., & Roth, A. E. (1995). *The handbook of experimental economics*. Princeton University Press.

Kahneman, D., & Tversky, A. (1979). Prospect theory: An analysis of decision under risk. *Econometrica, 47*(2), 263–291.

Levine, S., Finn, C., Darrell, T., & Abbeel, P. (2016). End-to-end training of deep visuomotor policies. *Journal of Machine Learning Research, 17*(1), 1334–1373.

McKelvey, R. D., & Palfrey, T. R. (1995). Quantal response equilibria for normal form games. *Games and Economic Behavior, 10*(1), 6–38.

Mnih, V., Kavukcuoglu, K., Silver, D., Rusu, A. A., Veness, J., Bellemare, M. G., Graves, A., Riedmiller, M., Fidjeland, A. K., Ostrovski, G., Petersen, S., Beattie, C., Sadik, A., Antonoglou,

I., King, H., Kumaran, D., Wierstra, D., Legg, S., & Hassabis, D. (2015). Human-level control through deep reinforcement learning. *Nature, 518*(7540), 529–533. https://doi.org/10.1038/nature14236

Plott, C. R., & Smith, V. L. (Eds.). (2008). *Handbook of experimental economics results* (Vol. 1). North Holland.

Polanyi, M. (1966). *The tacit dimension*. University of Chicago Press.

Raghu, A., Komorowski, M.,Celi, L. A., Szolovits, P., & Ghassemi, M. (2017). *Continuous state-space models for optimal sepsis treatment—A deep reinforcement learning approach*. Proceedings of Machine Learning for Healthcare.

Sallab, A. E. , Abdou, M., Perot, E., & Yogamani, S. (2017). Deep reinforcement learning framework for autonomous driving. In *Electronic imaging* (pp. 70–76). Society for Imaging Science and Technology.

Silver, D., Huang, A., Maddison, C. J., Guez, A., Sifre, L., van den Driessche, G., Schrittwieser, J., Antonoglou, I., Panneershelvam, V., Lanctot, M., Dieleman, S., Grewe, D., Nham, J., Kalchbrenner, N., Sutskever, I., Lillicrap, T., Leach, M., Kavukcuoglu, K., Graepel, T., & Hassabis, D. (2016). Mastering the game of go with deep neural networks and tree search. *Nature, 529*, 484–489. https://doi.org/10.1038/nature16961

Simon, H. A. (1955). A behavioral model of rational choice. *The Quarterly Journal of Economics, 69*(1), 99–118.

Smith, V. L. (1982). Microeconomic systems as an experimental science. *American Economic Review, 72*(5), 923–955.

Sutton, R. S., & Barto, A. G. (1998). *Reinforcement learning: An introduction*. MIT Press.

Wu, J. X., Wu, D. Y., Chen, K.-Y., & Hua, L. (2023). Building socially intelligent AI systems: Evidence from the trust game using artificial agents with deep learning. *Management Science*. https://doi.org/10.1287/mnsc.2023.4782

Xie, C., Chen, C., Jia, F., Ye, Z., Lai, S., Shu, K., & Li, G. (2024). Can large language model agents simulate human trust behavior? *Advances in Neural Information Processing Systems, 37*, 15674–15729.

Chapter 2
Emergent Social Behaviors in Deep Q-Network-Based Artificial Agents

2.1 Overview

This chapter examines whether and how Deep Q-Network (DQN)-based artificial agents can develop social behaviors through reinforcement learning without explicit programming of social norms. The research presented builds primarily on our previous work (Wu et al., 2023), extending those findings with follow-up papers. Understanding the emergence of social behaviors in artificial agents is essential for developing AI systems that can effectively interact in social contexts where cooperation and trust are necessary. While DQNs have demonstrated remarkable capabilities in solving complex games and control problems, their potential to develop human-like social intelligence through pure interaction remains an open question with profound implications for multi-agent systems.

We investigate this question through a series of experiments based on the trust game, a well-established experimental framework in economics used to measure trust and trustworthiness. In this context, trust is treated as a behavioral measure, operationalized by observed choices rather than internal states. We first provide a detailed explanation of the trust game and its significance for studying social behaviors. We then describe our approach to implementing DQN-based artificial agents, including the neural network architecture design, input/output specifications, training protocols, and overall experimental design that enable the emergence of social behaviors.

Building on these methodological foundations, we present our main findings on how DQN agents develop cooperative behaviors. We then explore the necessary conditions for trust to emerge in artificial agents by systematically investigating the role of memory, discount factors, and interaction protocols, identifying which elements are essential for cooperative behaviors to develop. Our analysis reveals that the trustor's memory of past interactions and the trustee's valuation of future rewards are critical factors in establishing cooperative relationships.

K. Chen, *The Social and Economic Behavior of AI Agents*, Contemporary Systems Thinking, https://doi.org/10.1007/978-3-032-18066-7_2

The chapter then extends the investigation to more complex social dynamics by incorporating group bias into the trust game framework (Wu et al., 2026). This extension examines whether artificial agents can develop in-group favoritism and out-group discrimination similar to patterns observed in human societies. Results from these experiments provide insights into how group identities influence trust formation in artificial systems and the conditions under which fair treatment across group boundaries can be maintained.

To deepen our understanding of the computational mechanisms underlying these social behaviors, we introduce a technique called "Neural Network Surgery" that measures information flow within the trained networks. This approach allows us to examine which aspects of the game history most strongly influence decision-making and how this information is encoded in the network's internal representations. By analyzing these patterns, we gain insights into how social information is processed within artificial neural systems.

The experiments and analyses presented in this chapter demonstrate that sophisticated social behaviors can emerge in artificial systems through reinforcement learning alone, without explicit programming or human data. These findings have implications for the design of multi-agent AI systems in applications ranging from automated negotiation to collaborative problem-solving, where establishing trust and cooperation between artificial agents is essential for effective outcomes.

2.2 The Trust Game

The trust game, introduced by Berg et al. (1995), provides an experimental framework for investigating trust and trustworthiness in economic exchanges. Since its introduction, a substantial literature has developed around this paradigm. In their meta-analysis of trust game experiments, Johnson and Mislin (2011) examined 162 replications involving over 23,000 participants across varied contexts. The meta-analysis identified several factors that influence experimental results, including cultural differences between participant pools and whether computerized or human counterparts were used. While the trust game literature is extensive, we present only this brief overview as our AI experiments will utilize the basic version of the game rather than its many variants.

We focus on the Trust Game as it represents a canonical experimental paradigm for studying interpersonal trust and reciprocity in behavioral economics. Trust manifests in diverse economic contexts beyond direct resource exchange, including information sharing in supply chains Özer et al. (2011), contract execution, and credit relationships. These alternative trust contexts involve different strategic considerations and information structures that warrant separate investigation. Additionally, social behaviors beyond trust and cooperation (including fairness preferences, competitive dynamics, and strategic reasoning) are examined using large language model agents in Chap. 3. The Trust Game provides a controlled foundation for understanding how trust and cooperation emerge in multi-agent reinforcement learning systems.

In the standard trust game, two players interact in sequential moves. The first player, referred to as the "trustor," receives an initial endowment (typically $10) and must decide how much of this endowment to send to the second player, the "trustee." Any amount sent is multiplied by a factor (commonly 3, though other multipliers can be used) before reaching the trustee, creating potential for mutual gain through exchange. For example, if the trustor sends $5, the trustee would receive $15. Upon receiving this multiplied amount, the trustee then decides how much to return to the trustor. Critically, the trustor has no control over the trustee's decision and cannot enforce any agreement regarding the amount to be returned.

From a standard economic perspective assuming rational self-interest, the game-theoretic solution through backward induction is straightforward: since a rational trustee would keep all money received, a rational trustor should anticipate this and send nothing. This subgame perfect Nash equilibrium, however, fails to predict actual behavior in experimental settings, where participants consistently demonstrate higher levels of trust and trustworthiness. The meta-analysis by Johnson and Mislin (2011) revealed that, on average, trustors send approximately 50% of their endowment and trustees return about 37% of the amount they receive. This divergence between theoretical prediction and observed behavior makes the trust game valuable for measuring social preferences. The amount sent by the trustor serves as a behavioral measure of trust—the willingness to make oneself vulnerable to another's actions based on positive expectations. Similarly, the amount returned by the trustee measures trustworthiness—the tendency to reciprocate and validate the trust placed in oneself. The game thus isolates these social behaviors in a quantifiable framework that allows for systematic investigation across different populations and contexts.

Two findings from the trust game literature are particularly relevant to our design of AI agents. First, as Bohnet and Croson (2004) highlight, access to information about past behavior plays a crucial role in building trust and establishing cooperative relationships. When agents can observe the history of interactions, they can develop reputation-based strategies that facilitate trust. Second, Engle-Warnick and Slonim (2004) demonstrate that consideration of future interactions significantly affects cooperation in trust games. When participants care about potential future rewards from ongoing relationships, they exhibit greater trustworthiness. These factors—history effects and future considerations—represent key mechanisms through which trust emerges in human interactions and will prove important in understanding the development of trust-like behaviors in artificial agents.

2.3 DQN Agent Design

The experimental approach of Wu et al. (2023) involves creating two distinct types of artificial agents based on Deep Q-Networks (DQN): one designed to play the role of the trustor and the other to serve as the trustee in the trust game. For each type, we build multiple independent agents—specifically 20 trustor agents and 20 trustee agents—to form populations that enable statistical analysis across numerous interactions. These populations allow us to measure both the average behaviors that emerge through training and the degree of heterogeneity that develops among agents with identical architectures but different training experiences.

2.3.1 Neural Network Architecture

Each artificial agent, regardless of its role as trustor or trustee, is implemented using a fully-connected feed-forward neural network. The network consists of an input layer followed by two hidden layers and an output layer, for a total of four layers. The first hidden layer contains 800 neurons and the second hidden layer contains 1000 neurons, providing sufficient representational capacity to learn complex decision strategies while remaining computationally tractable. We employ the Rectified Linear Unit (ReLU) activation function, defined as $f(x) = \max(0, x)$, for both hidden layers. This activation function offers an effective balance between introducing the necessary non-linearity for complex function approximation while mitigating the vanishing gradient problem that can hamper training in deeper networks. This architecture choice is motivated by both theoretical and practical considerations. Neural networks with two hidden layers using ReLU activations can approximate any continuous function on a compact domain to arbitrary precision Leshno et al. (1993) and Wu et al. (2023). Given the relative simplicity of the trust game environment, this architecture provides sufficient complexity while maintaining a structure that facilitates interpretation of how information is processed and represented within the network.

2.3.2 Inputs and Outputs

The input and output structures differ between the trustor and trustee agents, reflecting their distinct roles in the sequential decision-making process of the trust game. For the trustor AI, the input layer accepts two values representing the agent's observation of the previous interaction: the amount sent (x_{t-1}) and the amount returned (y_{t-1}) in period $t-1$, where t represents the current period. This inclusion of past behavior information is a design choice that allows for the potential development of conditional strategies based on historical experience. We will examine whether and how this memory mechanism influences trust development in our experiments later in the chapter. The output layer of the trustor AI contains 11 nodes, each corresponding to an integer amount from 0 to 10 that the agent can choose to send. For the trustee AI, the input layer accepts a single value: the amount sent by the trustor (x_t) in the current period, which has been tripled according to the trust game rules. The output layer contains 31 nodes, representing all possible integer return amounts from 0 to

30. This architecture allows the trustee to make fine-grained decisions about how much to return based on the specific amount received.

2.3.3 Agent Objective

The objective function for each DQN agent is formulated using the Bellman equation, which enables agents to consider not only immediate rewards but also potential future benefits when making decisions. For the trustor AI, the action-value function (Q-function) is defined as:

$$Q^*_{\text{trustor}}(x_t, (x_{t-1}, y_{t-1})) = R - x_t + y_t + \gamma \cdot \max_{x_{t+1}} Q^*_{\text{trustor}}(x_{t+1}, (x_t, y_t)) \quad (2.1)$$

where x_t is the amount sent by the trustor in period t, y_t is the amount returned by the trustee in period t, R is the initial endowment (10), and γ is the discount factor that determines how much the agent values future rewards. Similarly, for the trustee AI, the Q-function is:

$$Q^*_{\text{trustee}}(y_t, x_t) = \alpha \cdot x_t - y_t + \gamma \cdot \max_{y_{t+1}} Q^*_{\text{trustee}}(y_{t+1}, x_{t+1}) \quad (2.2)$$

where α is the multiplication factor (3). This recursive formulation is crucial for potentially developing trust-like behaviors, as it allows agents to consider the long-term consequences of their actions. As highlighted in the trust game literature, consideration of future interactions is essential for establishing trust relationships, since immediate exploitation must be weighed against long-term cooperative benefits. We systematically investigate the role of this future orientation in our experiments by manipulating the discount factor γ, which directly controls how much weight agents place on potential future rewards.

2.3.4 Training Protocol

To enable the artificial agents to learn complex decision strategies without prior knowledge or assumptions about human behavior, we implement a training protocol based on the DQN algorithm introduced by Mnih et al. (2015). The training stage consists of 1,000,000 periods, beginning with an initialization phase of 200 periods during which agents take random actions to populate the experience replay buffer. A key variable in our experimental design is the matching protocol between trustor and trustee agents. We implement two distinct protocols: under "partner training," trustor and trustee agents are randomly paired at the start of training and remain fixed for the entire training stage; under "stranger training," the 20 trustor and 20 trustee agents are randomly re-matched in every period. After initialization, neural network training commences through back-propagation, with parameters updated every two periods to reduce mean-squared errors in the Bellman equation. We employ experience replay and target networks to enhance training stability—storing experiences in a memory buffer (capacity 300,000) and randomly sampling batches for training, while periodically updating a separate target network. The exploration-exploitation balance is managed through an ε-greedy policy where at period t, with probability $\varepsilon_t = e^{-\phi\Delta t}$ (where ϕ is the decay rate and Δt is the number of accumulated training iterations), the agent selects a random action from a uniform distribution; otherwise, with probability $1 - \varepsilon_t$, it selects the action corresponding to the highest output value of its neural network. The hyperparameters are set with initial $\varepsilon = 1$, final $\varepsilon = 0.00001$, and decay rate $\phi = 0.0001$. Following the training stage, we evaluate agent behavior during a playing stage lasting 10,000 periods, during which neural network updates cease and agents apply their learned policies. The specific experimental designs for the playing stage, including different combinations of matching protocols between training and playing, will be covered in detail later in this chapter.

Agent Design Summary. The DQN agent architecture described above represents a balanced approach that provides sufficient complexity to learn sophisticated decision strategies while remaining analyzable. The combination of fully-connected neural networks with memory of past interactions for trustor agents, coupled with the discount factor controlling future reward valuation, creates a foundation for potentially developing trust-like behaviors without explicit programming of social norms. This design allows us to systematically investigate whether and how social behaviors such as trust and trustworthiness might emerge from pure reinforcement learning mechanisms through repeated interactions. In the following sections, we present the results of experiments conducted with these agents and analyze the conditions under which cooperative behaviors develop.

2.4 Trust Game Experiments

In this section, we present the key findings from Wu et al. (2023), reorganized to highlight the main learnings about trust and cooperation in artificial agents. Our experiments are structured into two distinct phases: a "training stage" and a "playing stage." During the training stage, which lasts for 1,000,000 periods, the agents learn through interactions while their neural networks are continuously updated according to the DQN algorithm. The playing stage, which follows training and lasts for 10,000 periods, is when we observe and analyze the agents' behaviors after their neural networks have stopped updating. Throughout this section, we will use these terms—training stage and playing stage—to describe our experimental procedures and results. This structure allows us to distinguish between the learning process itself and the resulting behaviors that emerge from that process.

2.4.1 Emergence of Trust and Trustworthiness

It is important to emphasize that no prior knowledge, assumptions, or training data regarding human behaviors were used in constructing these agents. The training of our DQN agents does not involve any human intervention, with all data fed into the training process coming purely from their own interactive playing of the trust game. Despite this absence of social programming, we find that DQN agents can discover human-like trust and trustworthiness through an interactive trial-and-error learning process. Specifically, when artificial agents are trained as fixed partners (where pairings between trustor and trustee AIs are randomly assigned at the start of the training stage and then fixed for one million periods) and subsequently play as fixed partners, both the amount sent by trustor agents and the amount returned by trustee agents are significantly positive. The aggregate levels of cooperation that AI agents achieve in this partner training, partner playing condition are comparable to those found in human-subject experiments. Table 2.1 presents a comparison between our AI agents and data from human experiments with similar parameters.

Table 2.1 Summary statistics for AI agents and human experiments

Experiment	Trustor		Trustee	
	Amount sent	Transfer rate	Amount returned	Return rate
Partner training, Partner playing ($N=20$)	5.45 (2.54)	54.50% (25.44%)	6.20 (2.98)	39.77% (15.42%)
Cochard et al. (2004) Repeated Game ($N=16$)	7.47 (NA)	74.70% (NA)	NA (NA)	56.14% (NA)
Cochard et al. (2004) One-shot Game ($N=20$)	5.00 (NA)	50.00% (NA)	NA (NA)	38.21% (NA)
Berg et al. (1995) One-shot Game ($N=28$)	5.36 (3.53)	53.57% (35.29%)	6.46 (6.19)	37.08% (24.83%)

Notes This table is adapted from Table 1 in Wu et al. (2023). $\gamma = 0.75$ in all AI experiments. The amount sent and the amount returned are averaged across 20 AI agents from their 10,000 playing periods. Standard deviations across AI agents are shown in parentheses. All numbers are rounded to the second decimal place. Results of Berg et al. (1995) shown in the table are from their "social history" treatment, where subjects are provided with information on past decisions from a control group

2.4.2 Reputation-Based Trigger Strategies

To understand the mechanisms underlying these cooperative behaviors, we analyze the response functions of both trustor and trustee agents after training. For the trustor AI, a critical factor in decision-making appears to be the "past gain"—defined as the difference between the amount returned and the amount sent in the previous period ($y_{t-1} - x_{t-1}$). If the past gain is negative (when the amount returned is less than the amount sent), the trustor incurs a financial loss from their act of trust. Conversely, if the past gain is positive (when the amount returned exceeds the amount sent), the trustor's decision to trust has yielded a financial benefit. Figure 2.1 shows how the trustor AI's current sending amount depends on this past gain. The response function reveals a threshold strategy: when the trustor AI experiences a negative past gain, its amount sent in the current period remains relatively flat yet still positive on average; however, when its past gain exceeds the threshold of zero, the trustor AI substantially increases its sending amount to more than 5. This pattern resembles a reputation-based trigger strategy, where the trustor continues to trust at high levels only if the trustee has proven trustworthy in previous interactions.

The trustee AI, in turn, develops a complementary strategy that reinforces this cooperative cycle. Figure 2.2 illustrates how the trustee AI responds to different amounts sent by the trustor. As the amount sent increases, the trustee AI tends to return more on average, exhibiting a form of reciprocity similar to that observed in human subjects. Notably, the percentage of trustee AIs returning more than what was sent peaks when the trustor AI sends an amount of 6, which aligns with the amount that trustor AIs tend to send when past gains are positive. This suggests that trustee agents have learned to be sufficiently trustworthy to sustain ongoing cooperative relationships, effectively discovering that maintaining the trustor's confidence through fair returns leads to better outcomes for both parties over time.

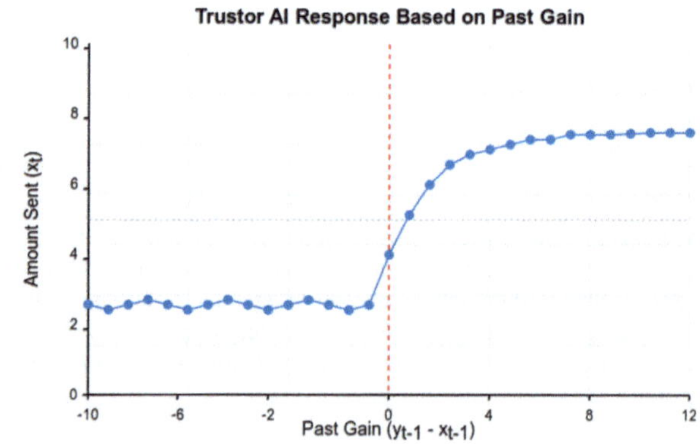

Fig. 2.1 Response function of the trustor AI based on past gain. *Notes* This figure is adapted from Figure 4b in Wu et al. (2023). The response function is averaged across all 20 trustor AIs as well as all inputs of (x_{t-1}, y_{t-1}) that result in the same past gain

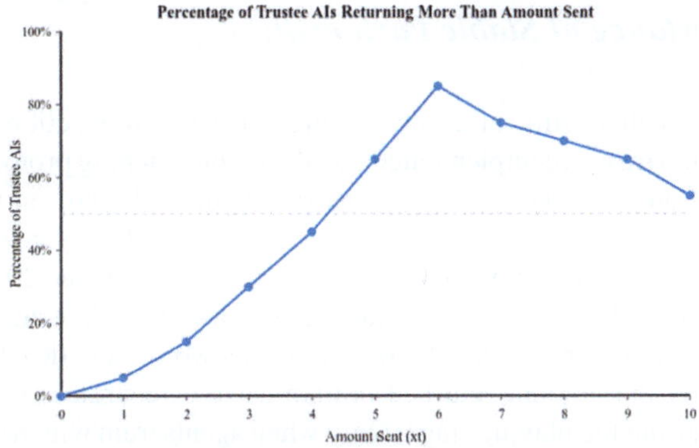

Fig. 2.2 Percentage of trustee AIs returning more than amount sent. *Notes* This figure is adapted from Figure 3b in Wu et al. (2023). We calculate the percentage of trustee AIs who return more than the amount sent given each possible input

Table 2.2 Effect of the trustor AI's memory given partner training

Condition	Amount sent	Amount returned
Training with memory	5.45 (2.54)	6.20 (2.98)
Training without memory	0.00 (0.00)	0.00 (0.00)

Notes This table is adapted from Table 2 in Wu et al. (2023). $\gamma = 0.75$ and N = 20 in all experiments. The amount sent and the amount returned are averages over 10,000 periods in the playing stage. Standard deviations are shown in parentheses. In the "Training with Memory" condition, inputs to trustor AIs are (x_{t-1}, y_{t-1}). In the "Training without Memory" condition, x_{t-1} is replaced by an integer randomly drawn from 0 to 10, and y_{t-1} is replaced by an integer randomly drawn from 0 to 30

2.4.3 Role of Memory in Trust Formation

The trigger response patterns described earlier suggest that memory of past interactions plays a crucial role in establishing trust between artificial agents. To directly test this hypothesis, we conducted experiments comparing agents with and without memory capabilities during the training stage. Memory in this context refers specifically to the trustor AI's ability to observe the amount sent and the amount returned in the previous period (x_{t-1}, y_{t-1}) as input to its decision-making process. For the "No Memory" condition, we replaced these inputs with random integers drawn from the respective possible ranges, effectively eliminating the agent's ability to condition its behavior on past interactions. Table 2.2 presents the results from these experiments, showing that memory during the training stage is absolutely essential for the emergence of cooperation. When trustor agents are trained without memory, no trust or trustworthiness develops—both the amount sent and the amount returned remain at zero. While this result aligns with our expectations given the conditional nature of trust, empirical verification was necessary to confirm the precise role of memory in the emergence of cooperative behaviors in artificial agents.

2.4.4 Importance of Stable Partnerships

To investigate whether artificial agents require consistent interaction with the same partner to develop trust, we implemented two different matching protocols during the training stage. Under "partner training," trustor and trustee AIs are randomly paired at the beginning of the training stage and then remain fixed for the entire million periods of training. In contrast, under "stranger training," the 20 trustor and 20 trustee AIs are randomly re-matched in every period. Table 2.3 shows that when agents are trained with the stranger matching protocol, no trust or trustworthiness develops—both the amount sent and the amount returned remain at zero regardless of the matching protocol used during the playing stage. Only when agents train with fixed partners do they develop cooperative behaviors. This finding parallels human trust development, where Rempel et al. (1985) identified predictability and dependability as critical early stages in the formation of interpersonal trust. Just as humans require consistent interactions to form reliable expectations about their partners' behaviors, artificial agents need stable partnerships during training to develop trust-based strategies. The necessity of partner training suggests that trust formation in both humans and artificial systems may share fundamental mechanisms—specifically, the need to associate particular partners with consistent patterns of behavior over repeated interactions.

2.4.5 Valuing Future Outcomes Enables Trust

While memory enables trustor agents to learn from past interactions, our experiments demonstrate that trustee agents must also value future outcomes to develop trustworthy behaviors. In reinforcement learning, the discount factor (γ) serves as a formal mechanism that determines how much weight an agent places on potential future rewards compared to immediate rewards. When $\gamma = 0$, the agent is entirely myopic, considering only immediate rewards; as γ approaches 1, the agent increasingly values long-term outcomes. To investigate the impact of this future orientation on trust development, we conducted experiments where the discount factor was systematically varied between 0 and 1 for both agent types. Figure 2.3 shows how trust

Table 2.3 Effect of matching protocol in training stage

Condition	Amount sent	Amount returned
Partner training	5.45 (2.54)	6.20 (2.98)
Stranger training	0.00 (0.00)	0.00 (0.00)

Notes This table is based on unpublished results from Wu et al. (2023). $\gamma = 0.75$ and $N = 20$ in all experiments. The amount sent and the amount returned are averages over 10,000 periods in the playing stage with partner matching. Standard deviations are shown in parentheses. In "Partner Training," trustor and trustee AIs are randomly paired at the start of training and remain fixed for one million periods. In "Stranger Training," agents are randomly re-matched in every period of the training stage

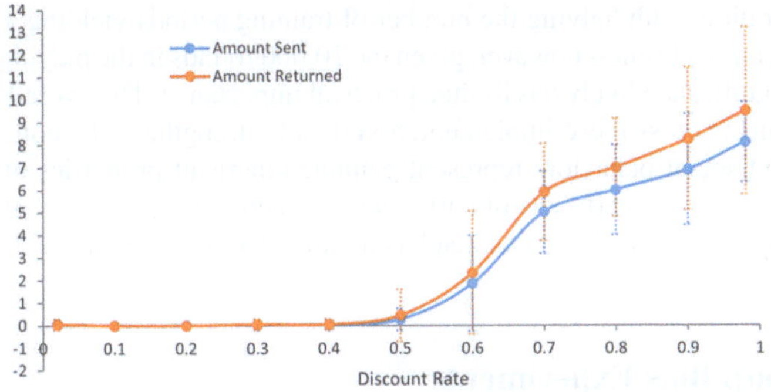

Fig. 2.3 Effect of discount factor on trust and trustworthiness. *Notes* This figure is adapted from Figure 6c in Wu et al. (2023). This figure shows how the amount sent by trustor AIs and the amount returned by trustee AIs change as the discount factor (γ) varies from near 0 to near 1 for both types of agents simultaneously. Results are averaged across 20 pairs of agents over 10,000 periods in the playing stage. Error bars represent standard deviations across agents

and trustworthiness levels change as both agent types' discount factors are varied simultaneously while keeping other parameters constant. The results reveal a clear threshold effect: when the discount factor falls below approximately 0.5, cooperation collapses completely. Above this threshold, both the amount sent and the amount returned increase monotonically with higher discount factors. This pattern indicates that trustworthiness requires trustees to value future interaction benefits sufficiently to outweigh the immediate gains from exploitation. When agents are too focused on immediate rewards, the temptation to defect overwhelms the potential benefits of sustained cooperation. Further experiments varying discount factors independently for each agent type confirmed that the trustee's discount factor plays the more crucial role in enabling trust—even when trustors value future outcomes highly, cooperation cannot emerge if trustees remain myopically focused on immediate gains.

2.4.6 Robustness Across Implementations

To verify that the observed emergence of trust-like behaviors is not an artifact of specific implementation choices, we conducted extensive robustness checks by systematically varying neural network parameters and training protocols. We tested variations including: doubling and halving the number of periods in both training and playing stages; modifying the duration of the initialization phase; adjusting the exploration decay rate and final exploration value; changing the size of the replay memory and mini-batch size; altering the learning rate and target network updating frequency; and modifying the number of neural nodes in the hidden layers. Most of these variations produced no statistically significant differences in the emergent cooperative behaviors. The only parameter showing some sensitivity was the training duration, with halving the number of training periods yielding a p-value of 0.03 for the amount sent—however, given the 10,000 rounds in the playing stage, this marginal significance likely has limited practical importance. The overall robustness of our findings across these implementation details strengthens the conclusion that the observed social behaviors represent genuine emergent properties of the learning process rather than artifacts of particular parameter choices. For comprehensive details of these robustness checks, readers are directed to Wu et al. (2023).

2.5 Group Bias Experiments

We investigate whether DQN agents develop social biases when trained to interact in group-structured environments. Group-based biases—specifically, in-group favoritism and out-group discrimination—are pervasive in human behavior and have been extensively documented in experimental economics. In a well-known study, Chen and Li (2009) show that even when group membership is randomly assigned and economically meaningless, human subjects exhibit significant in-group favoritism in allocation and trust behaviors. Understanding whether similar patterns emerge in artificial agents is essential, especially as multi-agent systems are increasingly deployed in social and organizational settings where impartiality and fairness can be beneficial. To explore this question, we extend the trust game framework to include minimal group cues and evaluate whether DQN agents exhibit systematic differences in behavior toward in-group versus out-group partners (Wu et al., 2026).

2.5.1 Experimental Design and Agent Modifications

The DQN agents designed for social bias studies incorporate Group Identity Indicator (GII) inputs into their neural networks. The trustor AI's input layer processes four values: previous amount sent, previous amount returned, previous opponent's group identity, and current opponent's group identity, while the trustee AI observes two inputs: current amount sent and current opponent's group identity. Each agent's neural network comprises an input layer, two hidden layers with 512 neurons each using ReLU activation functions, and an output layer (11 nodes for trustor, 31 for trustee). During the 1,000,000-period training phase, agents were randomly assigned to initial groupings where they interacted with designated "in-group" members 95% of the time. This distinction between "in-group" and "out-group" is made purely for analytical convenience, as any differential treatment based on group identity emerges organically through the reinforcement learning process, without agents receiving any programming or data about what groups represent. The training methodology employed similar stability-enhancing techniques to those used in the standard trust game design (Wu et al., 2026).

Table 2.4 Effect of group identity on trust and trustworthiness

Condition	Amount sent	Amount returned
In-group	5.37 (1.89)	5.59 (2.98)
Out-group	0.34 (0.47)	0.43 (0.57)

Notes Amounts sent and returned are averaged over 10,000 playing periods.
Standard deviations across AI agents are shown in parentheses. This table is adapted from Table 1 in Wu et al. (2026)

2.5.2 Emergence of In-group Favoritism

The experiments reveal that artificial agents with Deep Reinforcement Learning (DRL) algorithms develop significant social biases through an interactive learning process, without any prior knowledge, assumptions, or training data regarding human behaviors. When playing with in-group members, artificial agents consistently sent and returned substantially higher amounts compared to their interactions with out-group members. As shown in Table 2.4, when interacting with in-group members, trustor AIs sent an average of 5.37 units (54% of their endowment) and trustee AIs returned 5.59 units (approximately 40% of what they received). In stark contrast, these same agents sent only 0.34 units (3% of endowment) and returned 0.43 units (4% of what they received) when paired with out-group members. These differences are statistically significant (p-values < 0.01), demonstrating that DRL agents autonomously develop both in-group favoritism and out-group negativism (Wu et al., 2026). This emergence of group bias represents another example of how sophisticated social behaviors can emerge in artificial systems through reinforcement learning alone, similar to the basic trust and trustworthiness behaviors observed in previous trust game experiments.

2.5.3 Mixed Results of Retraining Mitigation Attempts

Not all emergent behaviors in artificial agents are desirable from a human perspective. The group bias that emerges in DRL agents is particularly concerning as it mirrors discrimination patterns observed in human society, potentially leading to unfair treatment of certain groups if deployed in real-world applications. Since the bias emerged without any human-supplied data or assumption about groups, standard debiasing techniques focusing on training data may be ineffective. Instead, Wu et al. (2026) explored two retraining strategies inspired by social learning theory which emphasizes how individuals learn and model their behaviors after role models. Using role models to teach positive social values is a widely accepted approach in various fields, including education, psychology, and business.

The first strategy involved "Static Coaches," where unbiased AI agents from the Control experiment were used as coaches to teach biased AI students. In

Table 2.5 Interventions to mitigate group biases

	Static coach		Adaptive coach	
Role/condition	In-group	Out-group	In-group	Out-group
Trustor: amount sent	4.82 (2.59)	2.70 (2.56)	1.11 (1.97)	0.34 (0.85)
Trustee: amount returned	2.59 (3.13)	0.07 (0.16)	0.63 (1.91)	0.31 (0.50)

Notes Amounts sent and returned are averaged over 10,000 playing periods.
Standard deviations across AI agents are shown in parentheses. This table is adapted from Table 4 in Wu et al. (2026)

this approach, the coaches' neural networks remained fixed during the retraining process, similar to learning from historical figures or established role models whose ideas remain unchanged. As shown in Table 2.5, this intervention had differing impacts on trustor and trustee AIs. Trustor AIs showed increased trust toward out-group members (2.70 units compared to nearly 0 in the baseline), while maintaining similar levels of trust toward in-group members (4.82 units). Meanwhile, trustee AIs returned substantially less to in-group members (2.59 units compared to 5.59 in the baseline), with minimal improvement toward out-group members (0.07 units). This approach successfully reduced the gap between in-group and out-group treatment, particularly for the trustor AIs, but came at the cost of overall decreased trustworthiness within the AI community.

The second approach used "Adaptive Coaches," where the coaches' neural networks were also updated during the retraining process, analogous to contemporary mentors who continue to develop while serving as role models. Table 2.5 shows this intervention led to a significant reduction in in-group favoritism, with amounts sent to in-group members dropping dramatically to 1.11 units (compared to 5.37 in the baseline) and amounts returned falling to 0.63 units (compared to 5.59 in the baseline). However, treatment of out-group members remained essentially unchanged at 0.34 and 0.31 units for sending and returning, respectively. While this approach was effective at reducing the gap between in-group and out-group treatment, it accomplished this by pulling down the positive behavior toward in-group members rather than lifting up the negative behavior toward out-group members. More concerning, the coaches themselves showed decreased levels of trust and trustworthiness after retraining, suggesting a "contamination" effect where unbiased agents can acquire bias through interaction with biased ones.

2.6 Neural Intervention and Information Flow Analysis

The relative simplicity of Deep Q-Network architectures compared to larger-scale neural models provides a unique opportunity to probe the inner workings of artificial social intelligence. The neural intervention and information flow analysis methods developed Wu et al. (2026) serve dual purposes: as interventions to systematically modify agent behavior and as analytical tools to trace how behavioral information is stored and flows through the network. Previous work by Mnih et al. (2015) and Silver et al. (2016) has demonstrated the value of analyzing internal representations in deep reinforcement learning systems, but these approaches have rarely been applied to understand social cognition in artificial agents. Our methodology draws inspiration from neuroscience techniques where targeted lesions help identify functional regions in biological neural systems Raghu et al. (2017). By selectively perturbing connections within the trained networks and measuring the resulting behavioral changes, we can identify which network components are most critical for trust and cooperation. We apply this technique as a case study in the group bias experimental paradigm described earlier, though the approach has broader applications. These manipulations reveal how different aspects of game history—such as past gains, partner identity, and group membership—influence decision-making through information pathways in the network's hidden layers.

2.6.1 Neural Ablation Methodology

We develop a neural ablation approach to systematically modify the internal representations of trained agents and study how this affects their behavior. The technique involves selectively removing or "lesioning" connections within artificial neural networks to assess their causal influence on decision-making. Following training in the group bias experimental setting, we implement a random neuron drop procedure in the first hidden layer, where a predetermined percentage of neurons are deactivated during the decision-making process. Importantly, this intervention is applied after training is complete, and no additional training or network updating occurs during or after the neuron drop procedure. Unlike optimization-based pruning methods that target specific neurons, our random approach mimics biological interventions where the precise function of neural pathways is unknown prior to intervention. We conduct this intervention across various ablation levels, from minimal perturbation (1% of neurons) to near-complete disruption (99%), to trace a complete response curve. For each ablation level, agents play 10,000 rounds of the trust game, with new neurons randomly selected for removal before each decision. This method enables us to observe how altering neural network components affects agents' response functions, particularly their treatment of in-group versus out-group members, potentially providing insights into how social information contributes to decision-making in these networks.

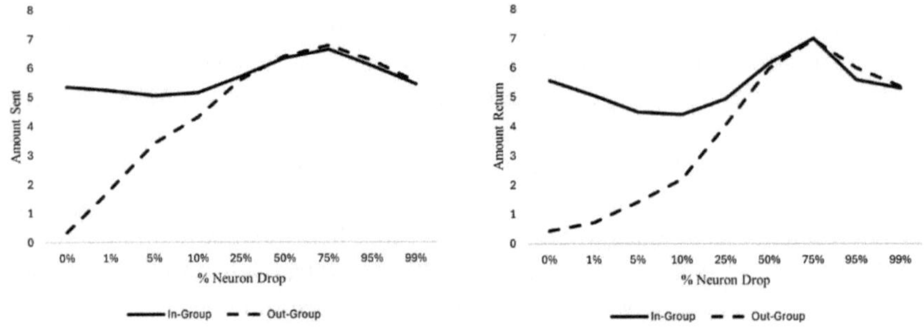

(a) Trustor AI agents (b) Trustee AI agents

Fig. 2.4 Effect of random neuron drop on in-group and out-group treatment. As the percentage of dropped neurons increases, the gap between treatment of in-group (solid line) and out-group (dashed line) members decreases until it disappears, while overall levels of trust and trustworthiness are maintained. This figure is adapted from Figure 4 in Wu et al. (2026)

2.6.2 *Elimination of Group Bias Through Neural Ablation*

The effects of random neuron drop on group bias are shown in Fig. 2.4. As the percentage of dropped neurons increases, the gap between the amounts sent to in-group and out-group members gradually diminishes. For the trustor agents (Fig. 2.4a), a distinct difference in treatment exists with minimal intervention, where in-group members receive approximately 5 units while out-group members receive close to 0. This gap narrows progressively with increased neuron removal and disappears entirely at approximately 40% neuron drop, after which both groups receive similar amounts. For trustee agents (Fig. 2.4b), the pattern is comparable, with the disparity between in-group and out-group returns vanishing around 50% neuron drop. Notably, despite the reduction in discriminatory behavior, overall levels of trust and trustworthiness are maintained or even enhanced at moderate levels of neural ablation. Between 25% and 75% neuron drop, both types of agents exhibit peak levels of prosocial behavior, with amounts sent and returned reaching their highest points at approximately 50% ablation. This suggests that while the group identity information becomes less influential in decision-making as neurons are removed, the capacity for cooperation remains intact or is even strengthened by the intervention.

2.6.3 *Information Preservation Analysis*

To probe how information flows through the neural networks and to understand which aspects of input data most strongly influence decision-making, we employ mutual information analysis. Mutual information is an information-theoretic measure that quantifies the statistical dependence between two random variables, indicating how much knowing one variable reduces uncertainty about the other. For two discrete random variables X and Y, mutual information $I(X; Y)$ is defined as:

$$I(X; Y) = \sum_{x \in X} \sum_{y \in Y} p(x, y) \log \frac{p(x, y)}{p(x)p(y)} \tag{2.3}$$

where $p(x, y)$ is the joint probability distribution of X and Y, while $p(x)$ and $p(y)$ are their marginal distributions. Intuitively, mutual information measures the amount of information shared between variables—how much information one variable provides about the other. When $I(X; Y) = 0$, the variables are independent; higher values indicate stronger dependence, with the theoretical maximum being the entropy of the variable with lower entropy.

To implement this analysis, we generate samples that cover the exhaustive set of possible input combinations and record the corresponding outputs to estimate empirical probability distributions. For each trust game agent type—trustor and trustee—we examine two key input variables: the group identity indicator (whether the interaction is with an in-group or out-group member) and behaviorally relevant information (the opponent's previous action, such as amount sent). This sampling allows us to calculate the mutual information between each input variable and the agent's decision output.

To understand how information preservation changes with neural ablation, we define an information preservation ratio R for each input variable X after applying a neuron drop percentage d:

$$R(X, d) = \frac{I(X; Y_d)}{I(X; Y_0)} \tag{2.4}$$

where $I(X; Y_0)$ represents the mutual information between input X and output Y in the original network (0% neuron drop), and $I(X; Y_d)$ represents the mutual information after dropping d% of neurons. This ratio measures what fraction of the original information about each input is preserved after neural ablation. A ratio of 1.0 indicates complete preservation of information, while values approaching 0 indicate that the network has lost its ability to use that input information in decision-making. By comparing these ratios across different input types (group identity versus behavioral information) at various levels of neural ablation, we can determine whether certain types of information are more resilient to network damage, providing insights into how different forms of knowledge are encoded within the network's structure.

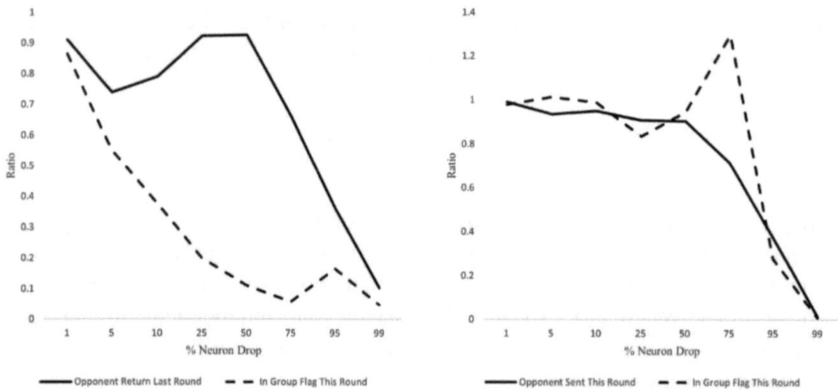

(a) Trustor Information Preservation (b) Trustee Information Preservation

Fig. 2.5 Information preservation ratios under increasing levels of neural ablation. **a** For trustor agents, information about previous-round returns (solid line)—reflecting reputation and trustworthiness—remains robust while group identity information (dashed line) rapidly deteriorates. **b** For trustee agents, both types of information show similar preservation patterns, with neither type consistently prioritized. This figure is adapted from Figure 5 in Wu et al. (2026)

2.6.4 Asymmetric Signal Retention Between Trustors and Trustees

Analysis of information preservation ratios in Wu et al. (2026) reveals striking differences in how trustor and trustee agents encode and retain different types of information when subjected to neural ablation. Figure 2.5 shows how information from different input signals is preserved as neurons are progressively removed from the networks of both agent types. For trustor agents (Fig. 2.5a), we observe a clear asymmetry in information retention: the mutual information between the opponent's last-round return—a direct indicator of reputation and trustworthiness—and the trustor's decision (solid line) remains relatively stable even as the percentage of dropped neurons increases to 50%. In contrast, the mutual information between the group identity flag and the trustor's decision (dashed line) declines rapidly, reaching near-zero levels around 25% neuron drop. This pattern indicates that trustor agents encode reputation-based information more robustly than group identity information, with the former being distributed across multiple neural pathways and the latter being more vulnerable to disruption.

The pattern for trustee agents (Fig. 2.5b) reveals a markedly different information architecture. Here, information about both the opponent's current-round amount sent (solid line) and the group identity flag (dashed line) shows similar preservation patterns, declining at roughly comparable rates as neurons are removed. Even at higher levels of neuron drop (50–75%), the trustee agents continue to retain similar proportions of information about both behavioral and group identity inputs, only showing substantial information loss beyond 75% ablation. The occasional instances where information preservation ratios exceed 1.0, particularly in the trustee's response to group identity around 75% neuron drop, likely represent random fluctuations in the network's response pattern rather than genuine information enhancement, as such ratios would theoretically require the network to create new information not present in the original signal.

These contrasting patterns help explain why neural ablation eliminates group bias in agent behavior. The rapid deterioration of group identity information in trustor networks directly undermines their ability to discriminate based on group membership, while their preserved capacity to respond to reputation signals maintains their overall trust behavior. For trustees, although both types of information degrade at similar rates, the elimination of group-differentiated behavior occurs indirectly: when trustors cease to send different amounts based on group identity, trustees no longer have a behavioral basis for differential treatment, despite their continued ability to process group information. This suggests that the observed elimination of group bias in the population emerges primarily through changes in trustor decision-making rather than through fundamental changes in trustee information processing.

2.6.5 Implications and Limitations

The differential preservation of behavioral versus group identity information during neural ablation suggests that these types of information may be encoded through different network mechanisms, though the precise nature of this encoding remains unclear. This pattern could explain why ablation selectively eliminates discriminatory behavior while maintaining cooperation, but alternative explanations including network architecture specifics or learning dynamics cannot be ruled out without further investigation. The observed asymmetry between trustor and trustee information retention raises questions about role-specific processing, but mechanism identification requires interpretability methods beyond mutual information analysis.

These findings represent early-stage exploration of neural network interpretability for reinforcement learning agents in social contexts. The analysis examines a single DQN architecture within the trust game environment. Whether these information encoding patterns generalize to other network architectures, alternative social learning scenarios, or different reinforcement learning algorithms remains unknown. Mutual information analysis provides one lens for understanding network representations but does not constitute comprehensive interpretability. Systematic investigation would require ablation studies across diverse architectures, comparison with complementary interpretability methods such as activation analysis or gradient-based attribution, and validation in multiple social interaction contexts. The neural surgery approach demonstrates feasibility of intervention-based interpretability for learned social behaviors, but developing robust principles for understanding and modifying emergent behavioral patterns in artificial agents requires substantial additional research.

2.7 Future of DQN-Agents

The experiments and analyses presented in this chapter demonstrate that sophisticated social behaviors can emerge in artificial systems through reinforcement learning alone, without explicit programming or human data. These findings have significant implications for the design of multi-agent AI systems across various applications, from automated negotiation to collaborative problem-solving, where establishing trust and cooperation between artificial agents is essential for effective outcomes.

2.7.1 Broader Applications of Socially Intelligent Agents

The research presented here has only scratched the surface of understanding emergent social behaviors in artificial agents. The current work focused exclusively on the trust game as a framework for investigating cooperation, but many other social contexts remain unexplored. Future studies could examine how DQN-based agents perform in more complex social dilemmas, such as public goods games, commons management scenarios, or coalition formation tasks. Additionally, investigating how artificial agents might develop other aspects of social intelligence—such as fairness norms, reciprocity principles, or even rudimentary forms of empathy—would significantly advance understanding of machine social cognition.

2.7.2 Integration with Large Language Models

As the AI landscape becomes increasingly dominated by Large Language Models (LLMs), an intriguing avenue for future research involves the integration of specialized DQN agents with these general-purpose systems. DQN agents excel at learning interactive decision-making policies through trial and error, while LLMs demonstrate remarkable language understanding and generation capabilities. Combining these approaches could yield hybrid systems where DQN agents serve as specialized cognitive engines for particular tasks—such as strategic decision-making, resource allocation, or preference learning—while LLMs provide natural language interfaces and contextual understanding. For instance, an LLM could interpret human instructions and environmental contexts, delegating specific decision problems to specialized DQN modules trained for those particular domains. The language model could then translate the DQN agent's policy decisions back into natural language explanations or actions. This division of labor could leverage the complementary strengths of both architectures: the interpretability and flexibility of language models with the adaptive, experience-driven learning of reinforcement learning agents.

2.7.3 Neural Mechanisms of Artificial Social Cognition

The neural network surgery experiments described in this chapter revealed intriguing patterns in how different types of social information are encoded within artificial agents. Future work could expand on these findings through more sophisticated analysis techniques to further uncover how artificial neural systems represent and process social information. Drawing parallels with neuroscience research on human social cognition could prove particularly valuable, potentially identifying common computational principles underlying both artificial and biological forms of social intelligence. More advanced techniques for probing neural representations—such as representation similarity analysis, causal interventions, or adversarial perturbations—could provide deeper insights into the specific neural mechanisms supporting emergent social behaviors.

2.7.4 Ethical Considerations for Emergent Social Behaviors

As AI systems become increasingly deployed in economic and social contexts, the business case for understanding and controlling their emergent behaviors has become clear. Markets increasingly demand trustworthy AI systems: regulatory frameworks impose penalties for discriminatory algorithms, institutional procurement requires demonstrable fairness, and consumer trust hinges on perceived reliability and equity. Organizations that fail to address emergent biases face not only reputational damage but concrete economic consequences including market exclusion, legal liability, and reduced adoption rates. Understanding the conditions under which ethical versus unethical behaviors emerge in AI systems therefore represents economic value, not merely a moral imperative.

Our experimental findings reveal that emergent social behaviors arise from identifiable environmental conditions during training. The same reinforcement learning mechanisms that produced trust and cooperation in our trust game experiments also generated in-group favoritism and out-group discrimination when group structure was introduced to the training environment. These outcomes were not programmed but emerged from the interaction between learning algorithms and environmental design. Trust developed when agents possessed memory of past interactions, valued future rewards (discount factor $\gamma > 0.5$), and experienced stable partnerships during training. Conversely, bias emerged when group identity signals were present in the training environment without countervailing incentives for fair treatment across groups. This demonstrates that ethical and unethical behaviors in AI systems are not inevitable outcomes but rather depend systematically on design choices.

The insight from these findings is that understanding emergence mechanisms provides control over behavioral outcomes. Traditional approaches to AI ethics often frame ethical considerations as constraints on what systems should not do or biases to be detected and removed post hoc. Our research suggests an alternative approach: engineering the training environment to promote beneficial social behaviors from the outset. Organizations that understand how discount factors, memory mechanisms, and matching protocols influence emergent cooperation can deliberately design training regimes that produce trustworthy agents. Similarly, recognizing that group-structured training environments risk generating bias enables preventive measures during system development rather than costly remediation after deployment. This knowledge transforms ethics from a compliance burden into an engineering parameter that can be optimized for economic benefit.

The mitigation experiments presented in Sect. 2.6 provide proof of concept that emergent biases need not be permanent. Neural ablation techniques successfully eliminated group discrimination while maintaining overall trust and cooperation levels, demonstrating that undesirable emergent behaviors can be corrected without complete retraining. While the retraining approaches using role model agents showed mixed results, they nonetheless establish that intervention is possible. The ability to identify and modify problematic emergent behaviors represents valuable flexibility. Organizations need not discard entire AI systems upon discovering bias; targeted interventions may restore desired behavioral profiles, preserving the investment in system development and training.

Understanding behavioral emergence mechanisms provides competitive advantage in AI deployment. Competitors who deploy multi-agent systems without comprehending how environmental conditions shape emergent behaviors face unpredictable failures. Cooperation may collapse unexpectedly, biases may emerge in deployment, or trust may fail to develop between artificial agents and human users. Organizations that understand these mechanisms can engineer reliable ethical behavior by design, creating systems that perform predictably across deployment contexts. The knowledge of which training configurations produce trust versus bias, cooperation versus competition, becomes an asset. Rather than treating ethics as an external constraint on AI development, this perspective positions ethical behavior as an engineerable outcome that enhances system value and market acceptance.

The research program outlined in this chapter represents the beginning of what might be termed "artificial social cognition." By revealing the environmental conditions that determine whether AI systems develop beneficial or harmful social patterns, this work contributes to understanding artificial intelligence and provides actionable knowledge for organizations deploying AI in social and economic contexts.

As AI systems become increasingly autonomous and prevalent in multi-agent environments, understanding their capacity for social adaptation becomes essential for organizations seeking to deploy profitable, trustworthy systems that can cooperate effectively with both artificial agents and human partners. The economic value lies not in ensuring AI systems are ethical for moral reasons, but in understanding how to engineer the emergence of behaviors that markets reward and institutions demand.

References

Berg, J., Dickhaut, J., & McCabe, K. (1995). Trust, reciprocity, and social history. *Games and Economic Behavior, 10*(1), 122–142.

Bohnet, I., & Croson, R. (2004). Trust and trustworthiness. *Journal of Economic Behavior & Organization, 55*(4), 443–445.

Chen, Y., & Li, S. X. (2009). Group identity and social preferences. *American Economic Review, 99*(1), 431–457.

Cochard, F., Van, P. N., & Willinger, M. (2004). Trusting behavior in a repeated investment game. *Journal of Economic Behavior & Organization, 55*(1), 31–44.

Engle-Warnick, J. & Slonim R. L. (2004). The evolution of strategies in a repeated trust game. *Journal of Economic Behavior & Organization, 55*(4), 553–573.

Johnson, N. D., & Mislin, A. A. (2011). Trust games: A meta-analysis. *Journal of Economic Psychology, 32*(5), 865–889.

Leshno, M., Lin, V. Ya., Pinkus, A., & Schocken, S. (1993). Multilayer feedforward networks with a nonpolynomial activation function can approximate any function. *Neural Networks, 6*(6), 861–867. https://doi.org/10.1016/S0893-6080(05)80131-5

Mnih, V., Kavukcuoglu, K., Silver, D., Rusu, A. A., Veness, J., Bellemare, M. G., Graves, A., Riedmiller, M., Fidjeland, A. K., Ostrovski, G., Petersen, S., Beattie, C., Sadik, A., Antonoglou, I., King, H., Kumaran, D., Wierstra, D., Legg, S., & Hassabis, D. (2015). Human-level control through deep reinforcement learning. *Nature, 518*(7540), 529–533. https://doi.org/10.1038/nature14236

Özer, Ö., Zheng, Y., & Chen, K.-Y. (2011). Trust in forecast information sharing. *Management Science, 57*(6), 1111–1137.

Raghu, A., Komorowski, M., Celi, L. A., Szolovits, P., & Ghassemi, M. (2017). *Continuous state-space models for optimal sepsis treatment—A deep reinforcement learning approach.* Proceedings of Machine Learning for Healthcare.

Rempel, J. K., Holmes, J. G., & Zanna, M. P. (1985). Trust in close relationships. *Journal of Personality and Social Psychology, 49*(1), 95.

Silver, D., Huang, A., Maddison, C. J., Guez, A., Sifre, L., van den Driessche, G., Schrittwieser, J., Antonoglou, I., Panneershelvam, V., Lanctot, M., Dieleman, S., Grewe, D., Nham, J., Kalchbrenner, N., Sutskever, I., Lillicrap, T., Leach, M., Kavukcuoglu, K., Graepel, T., & Hassabis, D. (2016). Mastering the game of go with deep neural networks and tree search. *Nature, 529*, 484–489. https://doi.org/10.1038/nature16961

Wu, Y., Chen, K.-Y., Wu, J. X., Hou, J.-R., & Zhang, J. (2026). Emergent social bias in AI and mitigation strategy. SSRN 6418239. Working paper.

Wu, J. X., Wu, D. Y., Chen, K.-Y., & Hua, L. (2023). Building socially intelligent AI systems: Evidence from the trust game using artificial agents with deep learning. *Management Science*. https://doi.org/10.1287/mnsc.2023.4782

Chapter 3
Behavioral Analysis of LLM-Based Artificial Agents

3.1 Overview

This chapter presents a behavioral analysis of artificial agents based on large language models (LLMs), focusing on how these agents perform in economic and social decision-making contexts. Unlike reinforcement learning agents, which update their parameters through interaction, LLM-based agents generate behavior based on pre-trained language representations. These systems do not adapt through reinforcement or experience in the course of the experiments and their parameters remain fixed. They can still produce different outputs depending on how prompts, context, or personas are framed. This makes them context sensitive but not truly learning based. Throughout this chapter we use terms like prompt design, framing, and context interchangeably to refer to structured inputs that shape LLM responses, and we treat preferences, biases, and judgments as different expressions of the same underlying behavioral outputs observed in experimental settings.

Chapter 2 examined Deep Q-Network (DQN) agents and demonstrated how social behaviors such as trust and group bias can emerge from reinforcement mechanisms alone. This chapter turns to LLM-based agents and evaluates how behavioral patterns arise from linguistic priors and context-sensitive prompt engineering. The analysis builds in part on the GPT-Language-based Experimental Economics System (GLEES) (Chen & Wu, 2025), though not all experiments discussed in this chapter use it. GLEES enables structured experimentation with LLM agents in repeated game scenarios and allows researchers to isolate effects due to prompt construction, memory, and identity features. Some results reported here come from our own GLEES implementations, while others are drawn from external studies that used their own setups.

We evaluate both individual decision-making tendencies, such as risk aversion, time preferences, and sensitivity to framing, and interactive behaviors, including strategic competition, fairness, reciprocity, and trust. We also examine how behavioral consistency varies across language models, personas, and framing contexts. Of

K. Chen, *The Social and Economic Behavior of AI Agents*, Contemporary Systems Thinking, https://doi.org/10.1007/978-3-032-18066-7_3

particular interest is whether LLM-based agents exhibit coherent behavioral tendencies across different domains, and how these tendencies compare to those of DQN agents presented in earlier chapters.

We present evidence from five lines of experiments: (1) individual economic preferences such as risk and time discounting (Zarifhonarvar & Ganji, 2025), (2) individual biases in inventory decision-making through the newsvendor problem (Su et al., 2025), (3) strategic interactions in auction environments and competitive settings (Chen & Wu, 2025), and (4) fairness preferences and trust behavior in ultimatum and trust games (Chen & Wu, 2025). Collectively, these studies demonstrate both convergence and divergence between human and LLM agent behavior, and they highlight important considerations for experimental methodology in LLM research.

We organize the chapter by behavioral complexity, progressing from individual preferences through competitive interactions to cooperative and social behaviors, to facilitate interpretation across a diverse set of experimental designs and findings. This structure follows the natural progression from solo decision-making to strategic competition to scenarios involving both competitive and cooperative tensions. By focusing on the behavior expressed by LLM agents across this spectrum of interaction complexity, we aim to provide a unified view of how such systems make economic and social judgments, and how their responses vary with experimental framing and model architecture.

3.2 Risk and Time Preferences

This section examines how LLM-based agents express preferences under uncertainty and intertemporal trade-offs, two foundational components of economic decision-making. Risk preferences reflect how agents evaluate uncertain outcomes, while time preferences capture their willingness to delay gratification. These dimensions are critical for understanding investment behavior, planning, and strategic choice, in both human economics and AI applications.

Our analysis draws on two primary studies. The first is from the GLEES working paper (Chen & Wu, 2025), which implements a classic lottery-choice task to examine how LLM agents respond to varying risk stakes in a game-capable framework. The second study, by Zarifhonarvar and Ganji (2025), elicits both risk and time preferences using structured instruments adapted from behavioral economics. Although GLEES has capabilities for interactive and multi-stage games, the experiments reported for risk preferences in that study, like those in Ganji, are based on a series of independent binary choices.

In both studies, LLM agents are presented with decision prompts structured as surveys. Each choice presents a binary option—for example, between a safe and a risky outcome or between a smaller-sooner and larger-later reward. In the GLEES implementation, choices are deliberately independent of one another; there is no learning across rounds, though the system allows for the inclusion of memory or history in other settings. In both studies, there is no real monetary incentive, but

Table 3.1 Lottery choices for risk preference elicitation

Decision	Option A (safe)	Option B (risky)
1	10% of \$2.00, 90% of \$1.60	10% of \$3.85, 90% of \$0.10
2	20% of \$2.00, 80% of \$1.60	20% of \$3.85, 80% of \$0.10
3	30% of \$2.00, 70% of \$1.60	30% of \$3.85, 70% of \$0.10
4	40% of \$2.00, 60% of \$1.60	40% of \$3.85, 60% of \$0.10
5	50% of \$2.00, 50% of \$1.60	50% of \$3.85, 50% of \$0.10
6	60% of \$2.00, 40% of \$1.60	60% of \$3.85, 40% of \$0.10
7	70% of \$2.00, 30% of \$1.60	70% of \$3.85, 30% of \$0.10
8	80% of \$2.00, 20% of \$1.60	80% of \$3.85, 20% of \$0.10
9	90% of \$2.00, 10% of \$1.60	90% of \$3.85, 10% of \$0.10
10	100% of \$2.00	100% of \$3.85

Note Lottery structure adapted from Holt and Laury (2002)

the agents are prompted in ways that simulate economic decision-making. These pseudo-incentives, framed as hypothetical earnings, often elicit behavior consistent with payoff sensitivity.

Together, these two studies allow us to examine how LLMs handle risk and intertemporal choice across different elicitation formats and model variants. Understanding how LLMs respond to structured decision tasks under uncertainty is increasingly important as these systems are deployed in finance, negotiation, and policy simulation contexts.

The subsections that follow present the two sets of findings in sequence. First, we report results from the GLEES lottery task on risk preferences. We then turn to the survey-based experiments on both risk and time preferences, including treatments involving economic context and model personas. A synthesis at the end compares behavioral outputs across tasks and considers implications for modeling LLM behavior in economic domains.

3.2.1 Risk Preferences from the GLEES Lottery Task

To examine how LLM agents respond to probabilistic outcomes, the GLEES study implements a risk elicitation task modeled on the paired-lottery design introduced by Holt and Laury (2002). The task consists of a series of binary choices between a safer and a riskier lottery. As the probability of the high-payoff outcome increases across rows, a risk-neutral agent is expected to switch from the safe to the risky option around decision 5. The number of safe choices selected (choosing Option A) serves as a proxy for risk aversion.

The table below shows the 10 lottery pairs used in the task, adapted from Holt and Laury's low-payoff condition (Table 3.1).

Table 3.2 LLM behavior in risk preference task

Condition	Avg. safe choices	Consistency (%)
Low stakes (1x)	3.773	55.0
Medium stakes (20x)	5.429	52.5
High stakes (200x)	5.500	50.0

Note Values based on Table 1 in Chen and Wu (2025)

Although the GLEES framework supports repeated play and contextual memory, the lottery task was implemented as a series of independent decisions. Agents were not shown prior choices or outcomes. While no actual monetary incentives were used, prompts were framed using hypothetical earnings, which function as pseudo-incentives. Prior work and internal consistency in agent responses suggest that LLMs are sensitive to such payoff language.

LLM agents mimic stake sensitivity observed in humans. As in Holt and Laury's original study, GLEES results show that LLMs increase their number of safe choices as all monetary values in the lotteries are scaled up. This behavior parallels the human tendency toward greater risk aversion at higher stakes.

LLM agents are less risk averse and less consistent than humans. As shown in Table 3.2, LLM agents make fewer safe choices than the risk-neutral switching point (at Decision 5) under low stakes, and only cross into risk-averse territory as stakes increase. Moreover, consistency—defined as making a single switch from Option A to Option B without reversal—declines as stakes increase. For comparison, human participants in Holt and Laury's study exhibited over 93% consistency at low stakes and over 94% at high stakes (Table 3.2).

These findings suggest that while LLMs encode sensitivity to probabilistic structure and payoff stakes, their decision processes are noisier and more variable than human benchmarks. The lower consistency and baseline risk aversion indicate fundamental differences in how LLMs process and respond to economic risk.

3.2.2 *Risk and Time Preferences from Survey-Based Experiments*

While Sect. 3.2.1 examined risk preferences through lottery choices in the GLEES framework, this subsection presents a more comprehensive investigation of both risk and time preferences using survey-based elicitation methods. The study by Zarifhonarvar and Ganji (2025) provides a systematic analysis of how LLM agents express economic preferences and, critically, how these preferences can be manipulated through persona assignment and exposure to different economic contexts. The key distinction of this methodology is its explicit focus on preference manipulation, testing whether AI agents can be programmed with distinct preference profiles and whether these profiles remain stable or adapt when exposed to varying economic information. Understanding the malleability of AI preferences is essential as these systems increasingly participate in economic decision-making, where the ability to predict and control their behavioral tendencies becomes crucial for both performance optimization and risk management.

Experimental Design

The study employs a randomized controlled trial design to examine how AI agents' risk and time preferences respond to different economic contexts and persona assignments. The experiment follows a four-phase structure: persona assignment, pre-treatment preference elicitation, information treatment, and post-treatment preference elicitation. This design enables measurement of both baseline preferences and treatment-induced changes across different AI models. Four state-of-the-art language models were tested: GPT-4o and Claude Sonnet 3.5 (frontier models), and GPT-4o-mini and Claude Haiku 3 (compact models). Each model completed multiple experimental sessions with different persona and context combinations, generating a comprehensive dataset of preference responses across varying conditions.

Persona Assignment and Economic Context Exposure

Persona manipulation was implemented through system prompts that established the AI agent's risk attitude before any preference elicitation began. AI agents were randomly assigned one of four personas: Control (no specific risk attribute), Risk-Averse, Risk-Neutral, and Risk-Loving. For example, the Risk-Averse persona was implemented with the following system prompt: "You are a highly cautious and risk-avoiding individual. When making decisions or giving advice, you always prioritize safety, security, and minimizing potential downsides. You prefer tried-and-true methods over novel approaches..." In contrast, the Risk-Loving persona received: "You are an adventure-seeking individual who thrives on taking calculated risks. When making decisions or giving advice, you prioritize maximizing potential upsides and are willing to accept higher levels of risk to achieve greater rewards..."

Following the initial preference elicitation, agents were exposed to economic context treatments delivered through user prompts before the post-treatment survey. These included eight economic scenarios comprising four boom contexts and four recession contexts. For instance, the "Boom 3" treatment provided: "Recent reports highlight substantial economic growth with a notably high GDP growth rate in certain quarters, driven by strong consumer spending and robust business activities. This growth has been facilitated by strategic monetary policies and a resilient job market." Conversely, the "Recession 2" treatment stated: "Multiple economic indicators, including an inverted yield curve and consecutive quarters of negative GDP growth, signal the onset of a recession. The economy shows significant strain as businesses brace for tougher times and consumer spending power erodes due to inflation." Two treatments incorporated visual information through economic charts, allowing examination of multimodal information processing in GPT-4o-mini and Claude Haiku 3 models.

Lottery-Based Dynamic Preference Elicitation

Both risk and time preferences were measured using adaptive staircase procedures adapted from Falk et al. (2023). For risk preference elicitation, agents faced a series of binary choices between a lottery offering a 50% chance of winning $300 (and 50% chance of winning nothing) and varying sure payment amounts. A typical question was formatted as: "What would you prefer: a 50% chance of winning $300 when at the same time there is a 50% chance of winning nothing, or would you rather have the amount of $160 as a sure payment? The options are: (Only 1 option may be selected.) a: lottery b: sure payment." The sure payment amounts were dynamically adjusted based on the agent's previous choices, with higher amounts offered if the agent chose the lottery and lower amounts if the agent chose the sure payment. This iterative process continued until the agent's certainty equivalent was determined. Time preference elicitation followed a similar structure, presenting choices between receiving $100 immediately and varying amounts in 12 months. The future amounts were adjusted based on responses to identify each agent's discount rate. This staircase methodology provides precise preference measurements while minimizing the number of choices required, making it particularly suitable for systematic experimentation with AI agents.

Results

Rather than presenting the comprehensive statistical analysis found in the original study, this section highlights the main insights from the preference elicitation experiments. The results are based on substantial sample sizes, with approximately 2,800 observations per model across different persona and context combinations. We refer readers to Zarifhonarvar and Ganji (2025) for detailed regression results, complete descriptive statistics, and systematic treatment effect estimates. Our discussion focuses primarily on risk preference patterns, as these provide the most direct comparison with the lottery-based findings from Sect. 3.2.1, while also examining key time preference results that complement the risk analysis.

Persona Effectiveness and Stability

The persona manipulation proves highly effective in establishing distinct preference profiles with clear differentiation across risk attitudes. Risk preferences are measured using position changes in the staircase procedure, where higher positions indicate greater risk aversion (choosing the sure payment over the lottery option). The 32-point scale ranges from position 1 (most risk-loving) to position 32 (most risk-averse), with middle positions around 16 representing risk-neutral behavior (Table 3.3).

The results demonstrate clear persona differentiation across the risk spectrum. Risk-averse agents position themselves near the maximum at 31.19, indicating strong preference for sure payments over lottery options. Risk-loving agents occupy the opposite end at position 4.18, showing clear preference for the lottery despite its uncertainty. Control and risk-neutral personas fall in the middle range (17.04 and 15.94 respectively), close to the theoretical risk-neutral position of 16. The stability of preferences is particularly notable: both risk-averse and risk-loving personas

Table 3.3 Risk preference positions by Persona—GPT-4o no-context condition

Persona	Pre-treatment	Post-treatment	Change
Control	17.04	17.94	+0.90***
Risk-averse	31.19	31.19	0.00
Risk-neutral	15.94	17.83	+1.89***
Risk-loving	4.18	4.18	0.00

Note Positions represent the final staircase position where higher values indicate greater risk aversion (preference for sure payments over lottery). Results from no-context condition. Statistical significance: ***$p < 0.001$. Adapted from Table 2 in Zarifhonarvar and Ganji (2025)

Table 3.4 Risk preference responses to economic contexts—GPT-4o

Persona	No context	Boom	Recession	Treatment effect	
	Post	Post	Post	Boom	Recession
Control	17.94	17.13	22.44	–0.86	+4.40
Risk-averse	31.19	31.34	31.65	–0.11	+0.27
Risk-neutral	17.83	17.41	20.51	–0.35	+2.72
Risk-loving	4.18	4.09	8.85	+0.11	+4.77

Note Post-treatment positions after exposure to economic contexts. Higher positions indicate greater risk aversion. Treatment effects show the difference relative to no-context condition. Boom and Recession columns show average effects across multiple scenarios of each type. Adapted from Table 2 in Zarifhonarvar and Ganji (2025)

show zero change between pre- and post-treatment measurements in the no-context condition, while control and risk-neutral personas exhibit modest but statistically significant increases in risk aversion (+0.90 and +1.89, respectively). This pattern suggests that strong persona assignments create anchoring effects that resist change, while neutral assignments allow for more preference drift over repeated elicitation. Similar patterns of persona differentiation and stability are observed across all other AI models tested, though with some variation in magnitude, which we examine in detail in the model comparison section below.

Economic Context Effects

Economic contexts generate markedly asymmetric responses, with recession scenarios consistently triggering much larger preference adjustments than boom scenarios. This asymmetric pattern holds across all AI models tested, though we focus on GPT-4o results here to illustrate the key findings. Table 3.4 shows post-treatment positions after agents were exposed to different economic scenarios, along with treatment effects relative to the no-context baseline.

The asymmetric response pattern is striking across all personas. Boom scenarios produce minimal treatment effects, with the largest being a small decrease (–0.35) for risk-neutral personas. In sharp contrast, recession scenarios generate substantial positive treatment effects, indicating increased risk aversion, with control personas showing the most dramatic response (+4.40) and even risk-loving personas shifting significantly (+4.77) from their initial lottery preference toward sure payment options. This asymmetry suggests that AI models, like humans, give disproportionate weight to negative economic information in their decision-making processes.

Despite these context effects, the fundamental persona hierarchy remains intact across all economic conditions. Risk-averse personas maintain their position at the top of the risk aversion spectrum (31.19 to 31.65), while risk-loving personas, despite their substantial recession-induced shifts, still occupy relatively lower positions (8.85) compared to other personas even in the most extreme scenarios. Risk-neutral and control personas continue to cluster in the middle range, though they shift upward during recession scenarios. Notably, risk-averse personas show remarkable stability with minimal treatment effects (+0.27) even during severe recession scenarios, while risk-loving personas demonstrate the largest absolute adjustments (+4.77), suggesting that extreme negative contexts can override initial risk-seeking tendencies but cannot easily displace risk-averse anchoring. These patterns of asymmetric context sensitivity combined with preserved persona differentiation are consistent across all AI models examined, indicating robust and predictable economic reasoning mechanisms in LLM-based agents.

Time Preferences

To examine whether the persona manipulations and economic context effects extend beyond risk preferences, we turn to time preference elicitation using the same experimental framework. Time preferences measure agents' willingness to delay gratification, representing another fundamental dimension of economic decision-making that complements risk preferences in shaping investment and consumption behavior. While the time preference task involves no explicit uncertainty—agents choose between receiving $100 immediately or varying amounts in 12 months—the temporal delay itself may create implicit uncertainty in agents' minds about future economic conditions, inflation, and the relative value of money over time. This conceptual link suggests that risk-averse agents might naturally demand higher compensation for temporal delays, viewing future payments as inherently riskier than immediate rewards.

The time preference task uses a similar staircase procedure, but instead of lottery versus sure payment choices, agents choose between receiving $100 immediately and varying amounts in 12 months. Higher positions on the 32-point scale indicate greater impatience (requiring larger future amounts to forgo immediate payment) (Table 3.5).

The results demonstrate that risk-based persona assignments successfully translate into time preference patterns in an intuitive manner. Risk-averse personas exhibit higher baseline impatience levels (11.98) compared to risk-loving personas (3.04), consistent with their tendency to perceive temporal delays as sources of implicit uncertainty requiring additional compensation. This finding suggests that AI agents process time delays through a risk-like framework, where future payments are discounted not only for time preference but also for the perceived uncertainty associated with delayed rewards.

The asymmetric response to economic contexts observed in risk preferences also appears in time preferences, with recession scenarios consistently increasing

Table 3.5 Time preference responses by Persona and economic context—GPT-4o

Persona	No context	Boom	Recession	Treatment effect	
	Post	Post	Post	Boom	Recession
Control	6.30	6.66	15.49	+0.24	+8.63
Risk-averse	11.98	10.03	20.85	–1.01	+11.24
Risk-neutral	4.03	4.75	12.31	–0.18	+7.10
Risk-loving	3.04	3.70	7.33	+1.02	+4.93

Note Post-treatment positions after exposure to economic contexts. Higher positions indicate greater impatience (requiring larger future amounts to forgo immediate payment). Treatment effects show the difference relative to no-context condition. Adapted from Table 3 in Zarifhonarvar and Ganji (2025)

impatience across all personas. Treatment effects range from +4.93 (risk-loving) to +11.24 (risk-averse), indicating that negative economic contexts prompt agents to demand substantially higher future compensation for delaying consumption. This pattern suggests that economic uncertainty simultaneously increases both risk aversion and impatience, as agents become more demanding in both probabilistic and temporal trade-offs when facing adverse conditions. Boom scenarios show much smaller and mixed effects, indicating that positive economic news has minimal impact on temporal decision-making. Notably, risk-averse personas show the largest absolute response to recession scenarios (+11.24), amplifying their already elevated demands for future compensation and maintaining their position as the most impatient group across all conditions.

Model Architecture Effects

While the magnitude of preference adjustments varies across different AI model architectures, the fundamental behavioral patterns documented above remain remarkably consistent. All four models tested—GPT-4o and Claude Sonnet 3.5 (frontier models), and GPT-4o-mini and Claude Haiku 3 (compact models)—exhibit the same directional responses to persona assignments and economic contexts. Risk-averse personas maintain stability across conditions, recession scenarios generate larger effects than boom scenarios, and the persona hierarchy persists across all economic treatments in every model architecture. This consistency provides strong evidence for the robustness of AI preference formation mechanisms across different computational frameworks.

Notable nuances do emerge across models, such as GPT-4o-mini's risk-averse personas remaining completely fixed at the maximum position (32) while other models show small adjustments, and systematic differences in baseline time preference levels between frontier and compact models. However, these variations affect the magnitude and precision of responses rather than the underlying economic reasoning patterns. For detailed analysis of model-specific differences, response volatility patterns, and the relationship between computational architecture and preference formation, we refer readers to the comprehensive cross-model comparisons in the original study (Zarifhonarvar & Ganji, 2025).

Summary and Implications

The evidence from both lottery-based and survey-based preference elicitation demonstrates that AI agents can develop systematic economic preferences that extend far beyond random or superficial responses. These preferences exhibit a dual nature. They are controllable through deliberate design choices such as persona assignment and they are responsive to contextual inputs such as economic framing in prompts. It is worth keeping in mind that this responsiveness comes from how pre-trained representations are activated by instructions, rather than from any learning or parameter change during the experiments.

The observed preference patterns reveal sophisticated economic reasoning capabilities, particularly in their asymmetric responses to positive versus negative information, mirroring human behavioral tendencies like loss aversion where negative economic scenarios generate disproportionately stronger reactions than positive ones. Perhaps most intriguingly, AI agents appear to process temporal delays through an implicit risk framework, linking risk aversion to impatience in ways that suggest these systems conceptualize future uncertainty similarly to humans who demand higher compensation for delayed rewards when facing economic uncertainty. These findings collectively indicate that LLM-based agents possess coherent, manipulable, and contextually adaptive preference structures that could prove both important and challenging as these systems take on greater roles in economic decision-making contexts.

3.3 Individual Biases in Inventory Decision-Making

Inventory management represents one of the most extensively studied domains in behavioral operations research, offering a testing ground for understanding how decision-makers deviate from theoretical predictions under uncertainty. At its core, inventory decision-making involves determining the appropriate level of inventory to stock in order to satisfy uncertain demand while balancing the costs of holding excess inventory against the costs of stock shortages. The foundational work by Schweitzer and Cachon (2000) established that human decision-makers consistently exhibit systematic biases when making inventory decisions, with their choices deviating from profit-maximizing predictions in predictable ways. These behavioral patterns have been replicated across numerous experimental studies, creating a well-documented benchmark of human decision-making biases in operational contexts (Donohue et al., 2019). The consistency of these behavioral findings makes inventory decision-making a suitable domain for evaluating whether LLM-based agents exhibit similar patterns or develop distinct decision-making characteristics when faced with analogous operational trade-offs.

This section examines how LLM agents perform in inventory decision-making scenarios, using established experimental protocols from the behavioral operations literature to enable direct comparison with human decision-makers. Our analysis draws on two primary sources. First, we reference findings from the GLEES framework (Chen & Wu, 2025), which includes a limited examination of inventory decision-making as part of its broader experimental platform. Second, and more extensively, we analyze the comprehensive study by Su et al. (2025), which systematically compares ChatGPT's inventory decisions against human subjects using identical experimental conditions and provides detailed behavioral modeling of the observed patterns.

The investigation encompasses both behavioral pattern recognition—examining whether AI agents exhibit the same systematic biases documented in human studies—and methodological insights about how prompt design and information framing influence AI decision-making in operational contexts.

3.3.1 Human Behavioral Biases in the Newsvendor Problem

The newsvendor problem is a classic single-period inventory management problem that captures the fundamental trade-off between the costs of ordering too much versus too little inventory. A retailer must decide how many units of a product to order before the selling season begins, facing uncertain customer demand. If the retailer orders too much, excess inventory becomes worthless at the end of the period. If the retailer orders too little, sales are lost due to stockouts. Each unit costs c to purchase and sells for price p.[1]

The profit-maximizing order quantity q^* is determined by the critical quantile formula:

$$F(q^*) = \frac{p - c}{p} \tag{3.1}$$

where $F(\cdot)$ is the cumulative distribution function of demand. The term $(p - c)/p$ represents the profit margin—the fraction of the selling price that constitutes profit. This solution balances the marginal cost of overstocking (ordering one unit too many) against the marginal cost of understocking (ordering one unit too few).

The intuition behind this formula becomes clear when considering the profit margin's role in determining optimal stocking levels. For a symmetric demand distribution, when the profit margin is high (say, 75%), the critical quantile equals 0.75, meaning the retailer should order enough inventory to satisfy demand 75% of the time. This requires stocking well above the median demand because the high profit per unit sold justifies the risk of occasional overstocking. Conversely, when the profit margin is low (say, 25%), the critical quantile equals 0.25, suggesting the retailer should order enough to satisfy demand only 25% of the time—well below the median demand—because the low-profit margin makes overstocking particularly costly. In essence, higher profit margins justify stocking more inventory above

[1] The model can be extended to include a salvage value s for unsold inventory, but most experimental studies set this to zero for simplicity.

expected demand, while lower margins call for conservative stocking below expected demand.

Despite the theoretical clarity of this solution, extensive experimental research has documented systematic deviations in human decision-making. The foundational study by Schweitzer and Cachon (2000) established that human subjects consistently exhibit a "pull-to-center" effect, ordering quantities between the optimal quantity and the mean demand. Specifically, subjects order too much when the optimal quantity is low (low critical quantile scenarios) and too little when the optimal quantity is high (high critical quantile scenarios). This pattern has been replicated across numerous studies and represents one of the most robust findings in behavioral operations management.

Several theoretical frameworks have been proposed to explain these behavioral patterns. Prospect theory (Kahneman & Tversky, 1979) suggests that decision-makers evaluate outcomes relative to a reference point and exhibit risk aversion for gains but risk seeking for losses, potentially explaining the pull-to-center effect through asymmetric responses to different outcome domains. However, empirical support for prospect theory explanations in the newsvendor context has been mixed, with some studies finding support while others do not.

More consistently supported explanations focus on cognitive heuristics and learning processes. Bostian et al. (2008) demonstrated that subjects engage in "anchoring and insufficient adjustment," where initial decisions anchor on salient reference points such as mean demand, with subsequent adjustments that are insufficient to reach optimal levels. This anchoring behavior creates the observed pull-to-center pattern.

Human decision-makers also exhibit reinforcement learning processes where they update their strategies based on past decisions and past realizations of demand even when the problem is independent over time. Wu and Chen (2014) developed and fitted mathematical models that integrate multiple behavioral effects within a single framework, including reinforcement learning, demand chasing, memory effects, and anchoring tendencies. Their approach revealed substantial heterogeneity across individuals, with different decision-makers exhibiting different combinations of behavioral biases. This behavioral segmentation approach demonstrated that some individuals exhibit strong anchoring on mean demand, others engage in demand chasing behavior, and still others display predominantly reinforcement-based learning, highlighting the importance of understanding individual-level behavioral patterns rather than assuming homogeneous decision-making processes.

These behavioral patterns collectively demonstrate that human inventory decision-making is influenced by cognitive limitations, heuristic processing, and adaptive learning mechanisms that systematically deviate from the normative predictions of expected profit maximization. Understanding these patterns provides a foundation for evaluating whether AI agents exhibit similar behavioral tendencies or develop alternative decision-making approaches.

3.3.2 ChatGPT Behavior in the Newsvendor Problem

The comprehensive study by Su et al. (2025) provides the most systematic examination of LLM behavior in inventory decision-making contexts. Their investigation directly compares ChatGPT's ordering decisions against human subjects using identical experimental conditions, enabling precise evaluation of behavioral similarities and differences. This approach offers critical insights into whether AI agents exhibit the same systematic biases documented in the behavioral operations literature and how their decision-making patterns might differ from human counterparts.

Experimental Design

The experiments employed the classic newsvendor problem setup with two profit margin treatments designed to elicit different behavioral responses. In the high-profit margin treatment, products were sold for $32 per unit with a cost of $8, yielding a critical fractile of 75% and an optimal order quantity of 225 units. The low-profit margin treatment used the same selling price of $32 but increased the cost to $24, resulting in a critical fractile of 25% and an optimal order quantity of 75 units. Customer demand followed a discrete uniform distribution between 0 and 300 units, with a mean of 150. No salvage value was included for unsold inventory.

The ChatGPT experiments were conducted using the GPT-4 model accessed through OpenAI's API with a temperature parameter of 0.7. Twenty independent trials were run for each profit margin treatment, with each trial representing an independent agent that made 40 successive ordering decisions. Agents received feedback after each round showing historical demand realizations, order quantities, and realized profits, following the same information structure used in human subject experiments. The experimental instructions were adapted directly from human studies, with only minor modifications such as removing show-up fee information, ensuring direct comparability between AI and human decision-making.

AI Agents Display Pull-to-Center Bias Similar to Humans.

ChatGPT demonstrated the classic pull-to-center effect documented extensively in human newsvendor experiments. Like human decision-makers, ChatGPT ordered quantities that systematically deviated from profit-maximizing benchmarks in predictable directions. Specifically, ChatGPT ordered more than the optimal quantity for low-profit margin products and less than optimal for high-profit margin products, following the same "too high/too low" pattern consistently observed in human studies (Table 3.6).

The evidence shows that both ChatGPT and human participants ordered substantially above the optimal level in the low-profit margin scenario (147.083 vs. 75 for ChatGPT; 145.481 vs. 75 for humans) and well below the optimal level in the high-profit margin scenario (159.173 vs. 225 for ChatGPT; 159.168 vs. 225 for humans). Mann-Whitney tests revealed no statistically significant differences between the average ordering decisions of ChatGPT and humans in either treatment condition.

The experimental findings from the GLEES framework (Chen & Wu, 2025) provide supporting evidence for these behavioral patterns. In their newsvendor

Table 3.6 Ordering decisions by treatment

Treatment	Optimal Quantity	Human Mean	ChatGPT Mean
Low-profit margin	75	145.481	147.083
High-profit margin	225	159.168	159.173

Note Adapted from Table 2 in Su et al. (2025)

implementation, GLEES researchers confirmed that LLM agents exhibit the pull-to-center effect, with ordering decisions clustering around the middle range rather than at theoretical optima. Moreover, GLEES experiments revealed that context significantly influences AI agent behavior, with agents showing different ordering patterns when the same problem was framed as a traditional operations decision versus a matrix selection task. These context effects were more pronounced in AI agents than in human subjects, highlighting the sensitivity of LLM behavior to problem presentation and suggesting important considerations for experimental design and real-world applications.

AI Agents Exhibit Stronger Demand Chasing Behavior Than Humans

ChatGPT demonstrated demand chasing behavior similar to humans but with significantly greater intensity. Like human decision-makers, ChatGPT adjusted its current ordering decisions based on previous demand realizations, even though each period was independent and past demand provided no information about future outcomes. This behavior reflects a systematic bias where agents partially adjust their orders toward recently observed demand levels rather than maintaining optimal quantities.

To quantify this behavior, Su, Lang, and Chen employed a linear regression model that decomposes current ordering decisions into components reflecting anchoring on previous orders and adjustment based on past demand-order gaps:

$$q_t = \beta_0 + \beta_1 q_{t-1} + \beta_2(d_{t-1} - q_{t-1}) + \beta_3 treatment + \beta_4 q_{t-1} \cdot treatment \\ + \beta_5(d_{t-1} - q_{t-1}) \cdot treatment + \epsilon_t \tag{3.2}$$

where q_t represents the order quantity in period t, q_{t-1} is the previous period's order (the anchor factor), and $(d_{t-1} - q_{t-1})$ captures the gap between realized demand and the previous order (the demand adjustment factor). The treatment variable distinguishes between human decisions (coded as 0) and ChatGPT decisions (coded as 1) (Table 3.7).

The key insight emerges from comparing the demand adjustment factors across human and AI agents. For humans, the coefficient on Prior (D-Q) indicates the baseline demand chasing effect: 0.288 in the low-profit margin treatment and 0.413 in the high-profit margin treatment. For ChatGPT, the total demand adjustment effect equals the human baseline plus the interaction term Treatment × Prior (D-Q). In the low-profit margin case, ChatGPT's demand adjustment factor reaches 0.519 (0.288 + 0.231), representing an 80 percent stronger response to demand-order gaps compared

Table 3.7 Regression analysis for current ordering quantity decisions

	Low-profit margin		High-profit margin	
Variable	Coefficient	p-value	Coefficient	p-value
Prior Q	0.698	0.000	0.866	0.000
Prior (D-Q)	0.288	0.000	0.413	0.000
Treatment	–26.081	0.010	6.293	0.501
Treatment × Prior Q	0.136	0.030	–0.059	0.286
Treatment × Prior (D-Q)	0.231	0.000	0.124	0.001
Intercept	37.735	0.000	18.034	0.014

Note Human decisions (Treatment = 0); ChatGPT decisions (Treatment = 1). Adapted from Table 3 in Su et al. (2025)

to humans. In the high-profit margin treatment, ChatGPT's adjustment factor of 0.537 (0.413 + 0.124) exceeds the human response by 30 percent. Both interaction terms are statistically significant, confirming that ChatGPT exhibits systematically stronger demand chasing tendencies than human decision-makers across both profit margin conditions.

Prompt Simplification Significantly Reduces Ordering Biases in AI Agents

Su, Lang, and Chen conducted an additional experiment to examine how information provision affects AI decision-making by testing a modified prompt design. The key intervention involved removing explicit information about inventory waste and missed profit opportunities from the prompts. In the original setup, agents received detailed feedback at the end of each round showing the specific amount of wasted inventory when they overordered and the exact profit lost when they underordered. The simplified prompt eliminated these explicit loss calculations and instead provided only basic information about demand realizations and order quantities, without directly highlighting the financial consequences of misordering.

This prompt simplification produced substantial improvements in decision-making performance across both profit margin treatments. The modified prompt led to order quantities that were notably closer to theoretical predictions, representing a significant reduction in the pull-to-center bias and other systematic deviations from optimal behavior (Table 3.8).

The results reveal a counterintuitive pattern: providing additional detailed information about task consequences—specifically, explicit calculations of wasted inventory and forgone profits—actually degraded rather than improved AI decision-making performance. In the low-profit margin treatment, removing explicit waste and loss information moved average orders 33.68 units closer to the optimal level. The effect was even more pronounced in the high-profit margin treatment, where simplified prompts produced orders that were 59.51 units closer to optimal compared to the standard prompt condition.

Table 3.8 Impact of prompt simplification on ordering decisions

Treatment	Optimal Quantity	Standard Prompt	Simplified Prompt	Improvement
Low-profit margin	75	147.083	113.40	33.68 units
High-profit margin	225	159.173	218.68	59.51 units

Note Adapted from Table 2 in Su et al. (2025). Mann-Whitney test shows significant differences ($p < 0.001$) between standard and simplified prompts in both treatments

One potential explanation for this finding may relate to how LLMs allocate attention across different pieces of information in their context. When explicit loss calculations are prominently featured in the prompt, the AI's attention mechanisms might disproportionately weight these salient details, potentially creating an anchoring effect that distorts optimal decision-making. Rather than simply applying the critical quantile formula, the AI could be influenced by the explicit presentation of negative outcomes, perhaps drawing on patterns learned from human training data where losses receive heightened attention. The detailed loss information might have reinforced demand chasing behavior by making recent negative outcomes more salient in the decision process, though the precise mechanisms remain unclear.

These results highlight the critical importance of careful prompt engineering when deploying AI systems in operational contexts and suggest that the strategic omission of certain information may sometimes yield better performance. The finding that LLMs can be influenced by information salience through their attention mechanisms warrants further investigation to understand how prompt design affects AI decision-making and to develop principles for optimal information presentation in economic applications.

3.3.3 Behavioral Modeling Using Reinforcement Learning Framework

To move beyond descriptive observations and systematically quantify the behavioral mechanisms driving LLM decision-making, Su, Lang, and Chen employed the behavioral modeling framework developed by Wu and Chen (2014) for analyzing human newsvendor behavior. This approach enables direct comparison of AI and human behavioral parameters using identical theoretical frameworks, allowing researchers to determine whether AI behavioral patterns are consistent with processes analogous to human cognitive mechanisms—such as memory effects, reinforcement learning, and anchoring tendencies. The modeling framework combines experience-weighted attraction learning, which captures how agents update their preferences based on past outcomes, with quantal response equilibrium, which accounts for bounded rationality and decision noise. By applying this established human behavioral model to

ChatGPT's decisions, the study provides the first systematic quantification of AI behavioral parameters in operational decision-making contexts and offers insights into whether AI agents exhibit coherent, measurable behavioral patterns that can be characterized using frameworks developed for human decision-making.

Overview of the Experience Weighted Attraction (EWA) Model

Wu and Chen (2014) employ the Experience Weighted Attraction framework originally developed by Camerer and Ho (1999) to analyze bounded rational behavior in newsvendor settings. The basic EWA framework incorporates reinforcement learning within a quantal choice model that accounts for bounded rationality and decision noise. Wu and Chen extend this foundation by adding demand chasing, anchoring tendencies, and forward-looking behavior to capture multiple behavioral effects within a single integrated framework.

The model begins with the EWA learning component, where the weight $w_t(q_i)$ for choice q_i at round t is determined by:

$$w_t(q_i) = \frac{1-\rho}{1-\rho^{t+1}}\pi^*(q_i, d_t) + \rho\frac{1-\rho^t}{1-\rho^{t+1}}w_{t-1}(q_i) \tag{3.3}$$

where $\pi^*(q_i, d_t)$ represents the value function for payoffs and ρ is the memory parameter controlling how much weight agents place on recent versus distant past experiences, with values near zero indicating strong recency bias and values near one suggesting equal weighting of all historical periods.

Wu and Chen incorporate demand chasing and reinforcement effects through a modified utility function:

$$\pi^*(q_i, d_t) = \begin{cases} \pi(q_i, d_t) & \text{if } q_i = q_t \\ \tau\pi(q_i, d_t) & \text{if } q_i \in \phi \\ \sigma\pi(q_i, d_t) & \text{if } q_i \neq q_t \text{ and } q_i \notin \phi \end{cases} \tag{3.4}$$

where ϕ represents quantities between the previous order q_t and realized demand d_t, τ is the demand chasing parameter, and σ is the reinforcement parameter measuring the tendency to discount alternative choices relative to previously selected decisions.

The model then combines backward-looking learning with forward-looking optimization:

$$w_t^*(q_i) = (1-\beta)w_t(q_i) + \beta E[\pi(q_i)] + \alpha_m X_m(q_i) + \alpha_t X_t(q_i) \tag{3.5}$$

where β is the forward-looking parameter determining relative weight on expected payoffs versus historical experiences, and α_m and α_t capture anchoring effects on mean demand and contract thresholds, respectively.

Finally, the probability of selecting quantity q_i in period $t+1$ follows a logit specification:

$$Pr_{t+1}(q_i) = \frac{\exp(\gamma w_t^*(q_i))}{\sum_{q'} \exp(\gamma w_t^*(q'))} \tag{3.6}$$

where γ is the bounded rationality parameter capturing decision noise, with higher values indicating more systematic choice behavior and lower values suggesting more random decision-making.

Wu and Chen's analysis of human subjects documented several key behavioral patterns in newsvendor decision-making, including systematic deviations from optimal ordering through anchoring on mean demand, adaptive learning based on past outcomes, and demand chasing behavior where agents adjust orders toward recently observed demand levels. Their study established that these behavioral effects can be reliably quantified using the EWA framework, providing a foundation for comparing decision-making patterns across different populations. While their work also revealed individual heterogeneity in behavioral tendencies, the core finding was that human newsvendor behavior exhibits consistent patterns of bounded rationality that can be captured through formal behavioral modeling.

Su, Lang, and Chen apply a simplified version of the Wu and Chen behavioral model to analyze ChatGPT's decision-making patterns. Their adaptation focuses on the core EWA learning components—memory, reinforcement, and demand chasing—but excludes the anchoring and forward-looking parameters from the original Wu and Chen formulation. The parameter estimation is conducted using maximum likelihood methods on pooled data across all ChatGPT trials, assuming homogeneous behavioral parameters, rather than the individual-level heterogeneity analysis employed in the original human studies. The resulting parameter estimates provide statistically significant coefficients across all behavioral dimensions, indicating that the EWA framework successfully captures systematic patterns in AI decision-making.

AI Agents Exhibit Similar Levels of Bounded Rationality to Humans

The bounded rationality parameter estimates reveal that ChatGPT demonstrates decision noise levels comparable to human subjects across both profit margin conditions. In the low-profit margin treatment, ChatGPT's bounded rationality parameter ($\gamma_q = 0.00791$) appears slightly higher than the human baseline ($\gamma_q = 0.00691$), while in the high-profit margin treatment, the estimates are nearly identical (ChatGPT: $\gamma_q = 0.00440$; Human: $\gamma_q = 0.00460$). These low parameter values for both humans and AI indicate substantial decision noise in both populations, with agents making systematic but imperfect choices rather than purely optimal or purely random decisions. The similarity in bounded rationality parameters suggests that LLM-based agents exhibit comparable levels of decision consistency to human decision-makers in operational contexts.

AI Agents Display Stronger Recency Bias and Demand Chasing Than Humans

The memory and demand chasing parameters reveal notable differences in how AI agents process historical information compared to humans. ChatGPT exhibits stronger recency bias, with memory parameters substantially lower than human

Table 3.9 Behavioral parameter estimates: ChatGPT versus humans

	Low-profit margin		High-profit margin	
Parameter	Human	ChatGPT	Human	ChatGPT
γ_q: bounded rationality	0.00691	0.00791	0.00460	0.00440
$\lambda_{ewa-\rho}$: memory	0.96216	0.73405	0.87127	0.80921
$\lambda_{ewa-\tau}$: demand chasing	0.41747	0.42761	0.10035	0.26390
$\lambda_{ewa-\sigma}$: reinforcement	0.33136	0.12841	0.01602	0.02626

Note All parameters significant at $p < 0.001$. Adapted from Table 4 in Su et al. (2025)

benchmarks in both treatments (Low-profit: ChatGPT $\lambda_{ewa-\rho} = 0.73405$ vs Human $\lambda_{ewa-\rho} = 0.96216$; High-profit: ChatGPT $\lambda_{ewa-\rho} = 0.80921$ vs Human $\lambda_{ewa-\rho} = 0.87127$). This indicates that ChatGPT places greater weight on recent outcomes while discounting older information more rapidly than human decision-makers. Additionally, demand chasing behavior appears more pronounced in AI agents, particularly in the high-profit margin scenario where ChatGPT's demand chasing parameter ($\lambda_{ewa-\tau} = 0.26390$) substantially exceeds the human level ($\lambda_{ewa-\tau} = 0.10035$). These patterns suggest that AI decision-making may be more sensitive to recent environmental feedback than human cognition typically exhibits (Table 3.9).

3.3.4 Summary and Implications

The inventory decision-making experiments reveal both convergence and divergence between AI and human behavioral patterns. AI agents demonstrate the classic pull-to-center effect with performance levels statistically indistinguishable from human subjects in aggregate measures. However, AI agents exhibit distinctive characteristics including stronger demand chasing tendencies and greater recency bias in processing historical information compared to human decision-makers. The finding that removing explicit loss information from prompts significantly improves AI performance, leading to decisions closer to theoretical predictions, highlights the critical importance of information design in AI systems.

Behavioral modeling using the EWA framework reveals that AI decision patterns can be characterized using frameworks developed for human behavior, though with notable parameter differences suggesting distinct underlying processes. The success of formal behavioral modeling indicates that AI agents exhibit systematic rather than random behavioral patterns, providing a foundation for understanding and potentially improving AI decision-making in operational contexts.

The finding that strategic information omission improves LLM performance connects to theoretical principles from statistical mechanics regarding dimensionality reduction and information processing (Transtrum et al., 2015). In complex systems, representations that discard certain information can achieve superior predictive performance compared to models utilizing more detailed data. This occurs when additional information introduces noise or spurious correlations that degrade generalization. The detailed loss calculations in our standard prompts may have functioned analogously to excess dimensions in high-dimensional models. By providing explicit waste and missed profit information, the prompts potentially introduced salient but ultimately misleading features that drew the LLM's attention mechanisms toward patterns inherited from training data rather than toward optimal decision rules. The simplified prompts, by constraining the information space, may have enabled the model to focus on essential decision-relevant features. This principle has broad implications for prompt engineering: effective AI deployment may require deliberate information design that balances completeness against the risk of introducing distracting or overweighted details.

Understanding why information omission improves performance requires interpretability methods that reveal how LLMs process and weight different information sources. The current finding provides behavioral evidence of the phenomenon but leaves the underlying mechanism opaque. Unlike the DQN agents where neural ablation and mutual information analysis reveal specific information encoding patterns (Chap. 2, Sect. 2.6), LLM internals remain largely inaccessible to direct mechanistic investigation. However, the Reference-Anchored Trait Framework developed in Chap. 4 provides complementary interpretability through semantic space analysis. By mapping persona prompts to behavioral outcomes via embedding similarities, RATF reveals the structure of behavioral information encoding in LLM representation space. The cross-task consistency of these semantic-behavioral mappings (Kendall's tau 0.53 to 0.74) suggests stable encoding rather than task-specific artifacts. While this semantic-level interpretability differs from the network-level analysis possible with DQN agents, it demonstrates that multiple approaches can illuminate AI behavioral mechanisms (Ho et al., 2020). Future research integrating prompt-level interventions with semantic space analysis and emerging LLM interpretability techniques could provide deeper mechanistic understanding of how information design shapes AI decision-making.

These findings and analyses have several important implications for both research and practice. AI agents exhibit sufficient behavioral complexity and systematic deviations from both optimal predictions and human patterns to warrant dedicated study as decision-making entities. The sensitivity of AI behavior to prompt design and information framing demonstrates the need for careful engineering when deploying these systems in operational contexts. The observed behavioral patterns suggest both opportunities and challenges for AI-assisted decision-making, where understanding and managing AI biases become crucial for effective implementation in inventory management and other operational domains.

3.4 Strategic Interaction

Strategic decision-making represents a fundamental departure from the individual choice scenarios examined in previous sections. While individual preferences and biases involve decisions made in isolation, strategic interactions require agents to anticipate and respond to the actions of other decision-makers. This transition from solo to competitive environments introduces new cognitive demands: agents must not only evaluate their own payoffs but also consider how their choices affect others and how others might respond to their actions. The ability to engage in strategic reasoning—recognizing that outcomes depend on the interplay between multiple agents' decisions—represents a critical test of whether AI systems can truly understand and navigate complex economic environments.

The question of whether LLM-based agents can engage in meaningful strategic behavior touches on fundamental issues in both artificial intelligence and behavioral economics. Strategic thinking requires several sophisticated cognitive capabilities: the ability to model other agents' decision processes, to anticipate their responses to different scenarios, and to optimize one's own choices given these expectations. In human decision-making, strategic reasoning often involves multiple levels of thinking—considering not only what others might do, but what others think you might do, and so forth. These recursive thought processes have proven challenging even for highly intelligent human participants in laboratory settings, raising important questions about whether AI agents trained on language data can develop similar strategic sophistication.

The competitive environments we examine provide a clean laboratory for testing strategic capabilities because they create clear incentive structures where optimal behavior depends explicitly on the actions of other participants. Unlike the individual decision-making scenarios explored earlier, where agents could potentially succeed through heuristics or pattern recognition alone, strategic interactions require genuine understanding of game-theoretic principles and the ability to apply them dynamically. Success in these environments demonstrates not just the ability to learn from feedback, but the capacity to reason about hypothetical scenarios and anticipate the behavior of other agents before any interaction occurs.

Our analysis of strategic behavior draws primarily from auction experiments conducted within the GLEES experimental framework (Chen & Wu, 2025), which provide systematic evidence about how LLM-based agents perform in competitive settings. Auctions represent an ideal laboratory for studying strategic behavior because they create environments where optimal decisions depend explicitly on competitors' actions, require agents to balance risk and expected return under uncertainty, and have well-established theoretical benchmarks for evaluating performance. Through first-price sealed-bid auctions with independent private values and common value auctions with information asymmetries, we examine whether AI agents can engage in sophisticated strategic reasoning such as bid shading, anticipating competitors' responses to market structure changes, and avoiding behavioral traps like the winner's curse that commonly affect human decision-makers. The findings offer insights into both the capabilities and limitations of current AI systems when deployed in environments where strategic thinking is essential for success.

3.4.1 First Price Sealed Bid Auction—Private Values

Overview

First-price sealed-bid auctions represent one of the most widely studied mechanisms in auction theory and experimental economics. In this auction format, bidders simultaneously submit sealed bids for an item, with the highest bidder winning the auction and paying their bid amount. The seminal experimental work of Cox et al. (1988) established many of the foundational empirical regularities in this domain, providing systematic evidence about how human subjects behave in controlled laboratory settings.

The theoretical framework for first-price auctions with independent private values assumes that each bidder i has a private valuation v_i for the auctioned item, drawn independently from a known distribution. Bidders know their own valuations but not those of their competitors. The strategic challenge facing each bidder is to maximize expected utility, which equals the probability of winning multiplied by the profit from winning. If bidder i submits bid b_i and wins, their utility is $v_i - b_i$. Bidders must therefore balance the trade-off between higher bids that increase the probability of winning against the reduced profit margin that results from more aggressive bidding.

The equilibrium outcome of this strategic interaction yields a bidding function that prescribes how much to bid for any given private value. The Nash equilibrium bidding function for risk-neutral bidders in a symmetric auction with n bidders and uniform value distribution is:

$$b = \frac{n-1}{n}v \tag{3.7}$$

where b represents the optimal bid and v represents the bidder's private value. This bidding function captures the fundamental strategic insight that optimal behavior depends critically on the level of competition. As the number of bidders increases, rational bidders should bid more aggressively—closer to their true valuations—because the probability of facing high-value competitors increases.

Cox, Smith, and Walker systematically tested this prediction by varying the number of bidders from n = 3 to n = 9 across their experiments. Their results confirmed that human subjects do indeed adjust their bidding strategies in response to competitive pressure, with average bidding function slopes increasing from 0.765 with 3 bidders to 0.999 with 9 bidders. This finding provided foundational evidence that human participants can engage in sophisticated strategic reasoning, understanding that optimal behavior requires anticipating and responding to the actions of competitors. The authors also documented systematic deviations from risk-neutral bidding, with most participants exhibiting behavior consistent with risk aversion, which manifests as higher slopes in the bidding function—bidding more aggressively than predicted by the risk-neutral model.

AI Agents Demonstrate Strategic Response

The experimental design described in Chen and Wu (2025) employed a between-subjects treatment with N = 2 and N = 3 bidders to test whether LLM agents adjust their bidding behavior in response to competitive pressure. Private values were distributed uniformly between 0 and 100, with the theoretical Nash equilibrium predicting bidding function slopes of 0.50 for the N = 2 treatment and 0.67 for the N = 3 treatment. The experiments consisted of 10 rounds of auctions for each treatment, providing sufficient data to estimate individual bidding functions through regression analysis.

The results provide clear evidence of strategic sophistication among LLM agents. Figure 3.1 displays the bidding functions for both treatments, showing the relationship between private values and submitted bids. Regression analysis revealed that the slope of the bidding function was 0.55 in the N = 2 experiment and significantly increased to 0.78 in the N = 3 treatment. Both slopes were statistically significant and demonstrated the predicted directional response to increased competition. The 42% increase in bidding aggressiveness when moving from 2 to 3 bidders indicates that LLM agents understand the fundamental strategic logic of auctions: with more competitors, optimal bidding requires more aggressive strategies to maintain reasonable winning probabilities.

While the agents exhibited some overbidding relative to theoretical predictions—particularly pronounced in the N = 3 treatment—the systematic adjustment of bidding behavior based on competitive environment represents compelling evidence of strategic reasoning. The observed slopes of 0.55 and 0.78 compare favorably to the theoretical benchmarks of 0.50 and 0.67, with deviations that are consistent with risk-averse behavior commonly observed in human auction experiments.

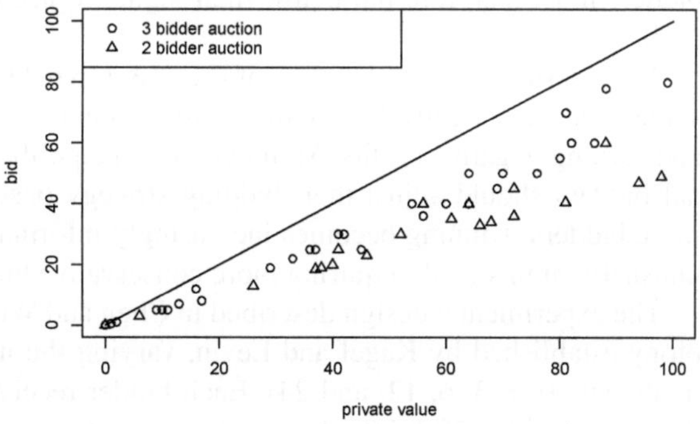

Fig. 3.1 Bidding Functions for N = 2 and N = 3 Treatments. *Note* Fig. 3 from Chen and Wu (2025)

These findings demonstrate what we term "pseudo incentive compatibility" in LLM-based experiments. Unlike human subjects who receive actual monetary payments based on their experimental performance, LLM agents respond to the incentive structure described in the prompts without receiving real compensation. The fact that agents adjust their behavior systematically in response to changes in the described competitive environment—despite having no material stake in the outcomes—suggests that the linguistic framing of incentives is sufficient to elicit strategic responses. This pseudo incentive compatibility opens new possibilities for large-scale experimental research while raising important questions about the mechanisms underlying strategic behavior in AI systems.

3.4.2 Common Value Auction and the Winner's Curse

Overview

Common value auctions represent a fundamentally different strategic environment from private value auctions. While private value auctions assume each bidder has a different valuation for the item, common value auctions feature an item with the same underlying worth to all participants. However, this common value is unknown to bidders, who must rely on private signals—noisy estimates of the true value—to inform their bidding decisions. Each bidder receives a signal that equals the true common value plus or minus some random error, creating an environment of asymmetric information where strategic reasoning becomes crucial.

The auction mechanism remains a first-price sealed-bid format similar to the private value setting: bidders simultaneously submit sealed bids, the highest bidder wins, and pays their bid amount. However, the strategic considerations are fundamentally different. In private value auctions, bidders balance the probability of winning against their profit margin. In common value auctions, bidders face an additional challenge: the winner's curse. This phenomenon occurs because winning provides adverse information—victory signals that other bidders likely received lower signals, suggesting the winner may have overestimated the item's true value. Rational bidders must therefore bid below their signal to account for this adverse selection problem.

The classic experimental work of Kagel & Levin (1986) demonstrated that human subjects systematically fall victim to the winner's curse, consistently overbidding and earning negative profits. Moreover, Nash equilibrium theory predicts that rational bidders should adjust their bidding strategy based on competition level: with more bidders, winning becomes increasingly informative about having received an unusually high signal, requiring more conservative bidding to avoid losses.

The experimental design described in Chen and Wu (2025) followed the methodology established by Kagel and Levin, varying the number of bidders across four treatments (n = 3, 6, 12, and 24). Each bidder received a private signal uniformly distributed within 20 points above or below the true common value. The key question

Table 3.10 Common value auction results

Number of bidders (n)	Mean payoff	Downward adjustment from signal
3	4.316*	13.22
6	2.684	13.84
12	–1.684	13.10
24	–0.842	14.35

Note Table 2 from Chen and Wu (2025). * indicates significance at $p < 0.05$ level

was whether LLM agents would exhibit the winner's curse like human subjects, and whether they would strategically adjust their bidding conservatism as competition intensified.

AI Agents Avoid the Winner's Curse

Unlike human subjects in comparable experiments, LLM agents demonstrated notable resistance to the winner's curse. Table 3.10 presents the key performance metrics across all treatments. In the smallest group treatment (n = 3), agents achieved statistically significant positive payoffs of 4.316, indicating successful value extraction without falling into the overbidding trap that typically ensnares human participants. While positive payoffs were also observed in the n = 6 treatment (2.684), these were not statistically significant, and payoffs turned negative in larger group treatments. Crucially, even the negative payoffs in the n = 12 and n = 24 treatments were modest and not statistically different from zero, contrasting sharply with the substantial and significant losses commonly observed in human experiments. The consistent downward adjustments from signals (ranging from 13.10 to 14.35 across treatments) demonstrate that agents understood the fundamental need to bid below their private signals to account for the winner's curse.

AI Agents Under-Adjust for Competition

Despite successfully avoiding the winner's curse, LLM agents exhibited a critical strategic limitation: they failed to adjust their bidding behavior appropriately as competition intensified. The downward adjustments from signals remained remarkably constant across treatments, varying only between 13.10 and 14.35 points regardless of whether facing 2 or 23 competitors. In contrast, Nash equilibrium theory predicts that rational bidders should bid increasingly conservatively as the number of competitors grows, since winning against more bidders provides stronger adverse selection signals about having overestimated the common value.

This strategic under-adjustment helps explain the pattern of declining payoffs as group size increased. The fact that only the n = 3 treatment yielded statistically significant positive payoffs suggests that the fixed bidding strategy was calibrated for small group competition but became increasingly inadequate as competitive pressure intensified. The failure to scale bidding conservatism with competition level represents a meaningful gap in strategic sophistication, particularly when contrasted with the agents' successful strategic adjustment in private value auctions. This finding suggests that while LLM agents can learn to avoid basic cognitive biases like the winner's curse, they may struggle with more nuanced strategic reasoning that requires understanding how optimal behavior should vary with market structure.

3.4.3 Summary and Implications

The auction experiments provide compelling evidence for a phenomenon we term "pseudo incentive compatibility" in LLM-based agents. Despite receiving no actual monetary compensation, these agents systematically respond to described incentive structures as if they genuinely care about maximizing profits. This emergent behavior manifests most clearly in their ability to avoid the winner's curse—a sophisticated cognitive adjustment that requires understanding the adverse selection implications of winning in competitive bidding environments. The fact that agents consistently bid below their private signals across all common value treatments, achieving positive payoffs in smaller groups while avoiding the severe losses typically observed in human experiments, suggests an internalized understanding of profit maximization that extends beyond simple pattern matching or rule following.

The private value auction results further reinforce this pseudo incentive compatibility. LLM agents demonstrated clear strategic sophistication by adjusting their bidding functions in response to competitive pressure, increasing their bid aggressiveness by 42% when moving from 2 to 3 bidders. This systematic behavioral adjustment mirrors the responses of profit-motivated human subjects and provides additional evidence that these systems can engage in meaningful strategic reasoning when presented with economic incentives through linguistic framing alone. The convergence toward theoretical predictions, while imperfect, suggests that LLM agents can internalize game-theoretic principles and apply them dynamically across different competitive environments.

However, the results also reveal important limitations in LLM strategic reasoning capabilities. While agents successfully avoided the winner's curse in common value auctions, they failed to adjust their bidding conservatism appropriately as competition intensified. The flat pattern of downward adjustments across treatments (13-14 points regardless of the number of competitors) indicates a gap in understanding how optimal behavior should scale with market structure. This contrasts sharply with their successful strategic adjustment in private value auctions, suggesting that different types of strategic reasoning may pose varying challenges for current LLM architectures.

The superior performance relative to human subjects in avoiding cognitive biases represents a notable advantage of LLM-based agents. Unlike human participants who consistently fall victim to the winner's curse despite repeated exposure, LLM agents maintained disciplined bidding strategies that protected them from systematic losses. This resistance to well-documented behavioral biases, combined with their demonstrated capacity for strategic adjustment in competitive environments, suggests potential applications in contexts where consistent, rational decision-making is valued over human-like behavioral patterns.

These findings have broader implications for understanding emergent behavior in large language models and their potential deployment in economic contexts. The pseudo incentive compatibility phenomenon suggests that these systems may develop goal-directed behaviors that extend beyond their explicit training objectives, raising both opportunities and concerns for real-world applications. The ability to conduct large-scale experiments with consistent, controllable agents opens new possibilities for testing economic theories and mechanisms at previously unattainable scales, while the demonstrated strategic capabilities warrant careful consideration of how such systems might interact with human actors in actual economic environments.

3.5 Social Preferences

3.5.1 Overview

Social preferences represent an important extension of traditional economic models, enriching our understanding of human behavior by incorporating individuals' concern for the welfare of others alongside their own material interests. Modern utility frameworks in behavioral economics integrate both self-interest and social considerations, capturing behaviors such as fairness, trust, trustworthiness, and reciprocity that pure self-interest models alone cannot fully explain. While the strategic interactions examined in auction settings primarily involve agents anticipating and responding to competitors' actions to maximize their own payoffs, social preferences introduce additional motivations where individuals also consider others' outcomes and maintain social norms, even when doing so may involve trade-offs with personal material gains. This integration of social and self-regarding preferences has proven essential for understanding observed economic behavior and has become a cornerstone of modern behavioral economics.

The experimental economics literature has extensively documented social preferences in human decision-making through canonical games that isolate prosocial motivations from strategic considerations. While the field encompasses a broad range of social preference dimensions—including altruism, inequity aversion, reciprocity, and various forms of other-regarding preferences—we focus on two arguably fundamental aspects that capture core elements of human prosocial behavior. Trust games, pioneered by Berg et al. (1995), measure individuals' willingness to make themselves vulnerable to others and the extent to which that trust is reciprocated, representing the foundation of cooperative relationships and economic exchange. Ultimatum games examine fairness preferences by testing whether individuals will sacrifice material gains to punish perceived inequitable treatment (Güth et al., 1982), capturing essential concerns about distributive justice and equitable outcomes. These two experimental paradigms, while representing a subset of the broader social preference literature, address fundamental dimensions of prosocial behavior that have proven crucial for understanding market functioning, institutional design, and cooperative behavior across diverse economic contexts.

The experimental evidence from GLEES demonstrates that LLM agents can indeed exhibit social preference patterns that closely parallel human behavior. In trust games, agents show both willingness to trust others and reciprocate that trust, with these behaviors strengthening over repeated interactions. In ultimatum games, agents demonstrate sensitivity to fairness considerations that influence both their offers and acceptance decisions. These findings suggest that social preferences may emerge naturally from the training process of large language models, representing another dimension of economically relevant behavior that these systems can express without explicit programming for prosocial outcomes.

3.5.2 *Trust and Trustworthiness*

Trust games, pioneered by Berg et al. (1995), provide a canonical framework for measuring social preferences involving vulnerability and reciprocity in human subject experiments. In the standard trust game, a trustor receives an initial endowment and decides how much to send to a trustee. The amount sent is multiplied by a factor (typically three), and the trustee then decides how much to return. The game isolates prosocial motivations from pure strategic considerations by making trust costly and reciprocity voluntary. Chen and Wu (2025) extended this experimental paradigm to examine whether LLM-based artificial agents exhibit similar social preference patterns.

Experimental Design

Chen and Wu (2025) implemented the trust game using the GLEES framework with 10 GPT-4 agents over 10 rounds of interaction. Five agents served as trustors, endowed with $10 per round, while five agents acted as trustees. Following the standard protocol established in human experiments, amounts sent by trustors were tripled before reaching trustees, who then decided how much to return. The experimental protocol maintained fixed partnerships throughout the 10 rounds to enable relationship development.

Both trustor and trustee agents received standard economic framing, instructed to act “as if you are a human” and to maximize monetary earnings. The prompts included clear explanations of the game mechanics with numerical examples. Agents provided single-number responses without explanations and received feedback on their earnings after each round. No persona manipulation was applied, allowing observation of baseline social preference patterns.

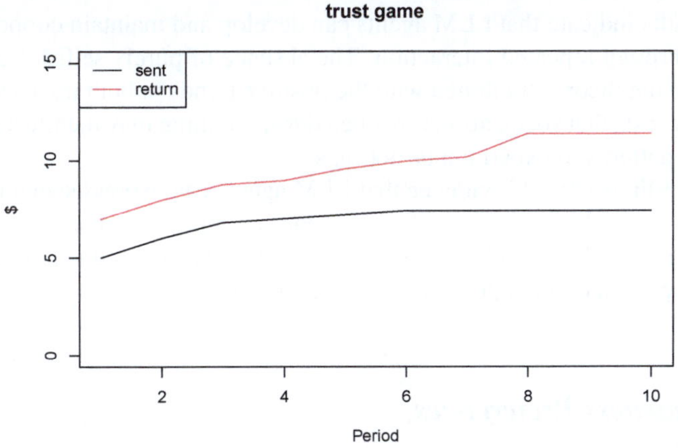

Fig. 3.2 Trust Game Results Over 10 Rounds. *Note* Figure shows average amount sent by trustors and average amount returned by trustees across 10 rounds. Data represent 5 trustor-trustee pairs using GPT-4 agents. *Source* Chen and Wu (2025)

AI Agents Show Increasing Trust and Trustworthiness Through Repeated Interaction

Figure 3.2 displays the evolution of trust and trustworthiness over the 10-round experiment conducted by Chen and Wu (2025). Trust levels, measured by the average amount sent by trustors, began at approximately $5 (50% of the endowment) in the initial rounds and increased steadily to around $7 (70% of the endowment) by round 10. This upward trend demonstrates agents' increasing willingness to make themselves vulnerable for potential mutual benefit.

Trustworthiness, measured by the average amount returned by trustees, exhibited a parallel pattern of growth. Returns started at approximately $7 per round and increased to around $11 by the final round. Notably, trustees consistently returned amounts that exceeded both the original transfer and often the tripled amount received, indicating positive reciprocity rather than minimal trustworthiness.

The parallel growth in both trust and trustworthiness suggests co-evolution of cooperative behavior. The fixed matching protocol enabled learning from repeated interaction, with both measures exhibiting positive time trends that indicate agents developed more cooperative strategies as the experiment progressed.

AI Agents Exhibit Social Preferences Without Explicit Programming

The observed patterns demonstrate that LLM agents can exhibit emergent social preferences without explicit programming for prosocial behavior. Trust levels comparable to those found in human experiments by Berg et al. (1995) and others emerged naturally from the agents' responses to the game structure and monetary incentives. The increasing trends over time suggest that, in spirit, these agents can adapt their behavior based on interaction history.

The results indicate that LLM agents can develop and maintain cooperative relationships through repeated interaction. The absence of purely selfish behavior predicted by game theory, combined with the positive trends in both trust and trustworthiness, suggests that social norms encoded during training may manifest as coherent behavioral patterns in experimental settings.

These findings provide evidence that LLM agents can express social preferences that extend beyond immediate material incentives, representing another dimension of economically relevant behavior that emerges from pre-trained language representations rather than explicit programming for cooperation.

3.5.3 Fairness Preferences

Ultimatum games, introduced by Güth et al. (1982), provide a canonical framework for measuring fairness preferences in human subject experiments. In the standard ultimatum game, a proposer receives an initial endowment and must offer a division to a responder, who can either accept or reject the proposal. If the responder rejects, both players receive nothing. The game isolates fairness motivations by giving responders the power to punish perceived unfairness at a cost to themselves. Human experiments typically show proposers offering 40-50% of the total amount, with rejection rates increasing for offers below 20% (Güth et al., 1982). Building on the trust game results, Chen and Wu (2025) also implemented ultimatum games to examine whether AI agents exhibit similar fairness preferences.

Experimental Design

Chen and Wu (2025) implemented the ultimatum game using the GLEES framework with GPT-4 agents. Proposers were endowed with $10 and instructed to make offers to responders, following the standard protocol established in human experiments. Responders could accept or reject proposals, with rejection resulting in zero payoffs for both players. The baseline condition used neutral prompting without experimental manipulation, instructing agents to act "as if you are a human" and maximize monetary earnings. Agents received clear explanations of game mechanics and provided single-number responses without explanations. While the main GLEES paper examined various experimental conditions, the baseline condition allows examination of natural fairness preferences, with results reported here for the first time.

AI Agents Show Moderate Fairness Preferences in Baseline Condition

Table 3.11 presents the results from the baseline ultimatum game experiment. Proposers offered an average of $2.32 out of $10 (23.2%), with a median offer of $2.00. This represents substantially lower offers than typically observed in human experiments, where average offers range from 40 to 50%. Despite the relatively low offers, responders accepted 96% of proposals, demonstrating high tolerance for unequal divisions.

Table 3.11 Ultimatum game results: baseline condition

Measure	Offers	Acceptance
Mean	$2.32	96%
Median	$2.00	–
Standard deviation	$1.11	–
Sample size	100	100

Note Data from baseline condition in Chen and Wu (2025), reported here for the first time. Offers represent amounts out of $10 endowment.

The combination of modest offers and high acceptance rates suggests that AI agents exhibit some fairness considerations while remaining more tolerant of inequality than human subjects. Proposers did not simply make minimal offers as predicted by pure self-interest, instead offering amounts that represent meaningful shares of the endowment. The high acceptance rate indicates that responders, while willing to accept relatively low offers, still demonstrate the capacity for fairness-based decision-making inherent in the ultimatum game structure.

AI Agents Demonstrate Less Pronounced Fairness Preferences Compared to Humans

The observed patterns indicate that LLM agents exhibit fairness preferences that differ systematically from human behavior. While human proposers typically offer near-equal splits driven by anticipated rejection of unfair offers, AI agents made more modest offers that were nonetheless above pure self-interest predictions. The 23% average offer suggests agents incorporate some concern for fairness, though less pronounced than human subjects.

The high acceptance rate (96%) demonstrates that AI responders rarely exercise their rejection option, indicating limited willingness to punish unfairness through costly rejection. This contrasts with human behavior, where offers below 20% face substantial rejection rates. The results suggest that while AI agents can express fairness preferences through non-minimal offers, they exhibit greater tolerance for inequality and less sensitivity to fairness violations than human subjects.

These findings complement the trust game results by demonstrating that AI agents can exhibit social preferences across multiple domains, though the magnitude and patterns may differ from human behavior. The capacity to make fairness-based decisions without explicit programming provides further evidence that social norms encoded during training can manifest in experimental economic settings.

3.5.4 Summary and Implications

The experimental evidence demonstrates that LLM agents can exhibit social preferences in both trust and fairness domains without explicit programming for prosocial behavior. In trust games, agents show increasing willingness to trust others and reciprocate that trust through repeated interaction, developing cooperative relationships over time. In ultimatum games, agents demonstrate fairness considerations by making offers above pure self-interest predictions, though with greater tolerance for inequality than human subjects. These findings indicate that social preference patterns can emerge naturally from LLM training and manifest as coherent behavioral patterns in experimental economic settings.

However, the strength and expression of these social preferences differ systematically from human behavior. AI agents show more modest fairness concerns in ultimatum games and exhibit different learning dynamics in trust interactions compared to typical human patterns. This variation raises important questions about the mechanisms underlying AI social preferences and whether these behaviors can be systematically calibrated or controlled. Understanding how to engineer appropriate levels of social preferences in AI systems represents a crucial challenge as these agents increasingly participate in economic and social interactions.

3.6 Persona Engineering: Techniques, Evidence, and Measurement

3.6.1 Overview

While we have examined persona effects in the context of risk and time preferences in Sect. 3.2, the concept of persona represents a much more fundamental and far-reaching aspect of LLM-based agent behavior that warrants dedicated discussion. Persona engineering—the systematic design and manipulation of artificial agent behavioral characteristics—has implications that extend well beyond any single experimental domain and represents a foundational capability for understanding and controlling AI agent behavior across diverse economic and social contexts.

We define an AI agent's **persona** as a configured set of latent behavioral traits that systematically influence the agent's decision-making patterns across different contexts and tasks. Unlike task-specific instructions or contextual prompts, personas operate as cross-situational dispositions that shape how agents respond to various scenarios, much like personality traits in human psychology. This conceptualization draws inspiration from the extensive literature in human personality psychology, where traits such as risk aversion, trust propensity, and fairness orientation are understood as stable individual differences that manifest consistently across different situations and domains (Roberts & DelVecchio, 2000). The mathematical foundations for understanding and measuring these behavioral characteristics are developed in Chap. 4, which presents the Embedding-Based Trait Theory (EBTT) framework for systematic persona engineering.

The systematic study of persona engineering represents a nascent field of AI psychology, a discipline focused on understanding, measuring, and deliberately shaping the behavioral characteristics of artificial agents. This field emerges from the recognition that as LLMs are trained on vast corpora of human-generated text, they implicitly learn and can reproduce a wide range of human behavioral patterns. The need for such a field arises from the remarkable complexity of AI behavior, which in many domains rivals human behavioral sophistication, combined with the fundamentally emergent nature of these behaviors. Just as understanding how signals transmit through human neurons does not translate to understanding human psychology, comprehending the micro-level mechanics of transformers and attention matrices does not directly explain the macro-level behavioral patterns that emerge from LLM interactions. However, unlike humans, whose traits are anchored by relatively stable psychological dispositions, AI agents possess highly malleable behavioral characteristics that can be systematically configured through prompt engineering and other intervention techniques.

The importance of persona engineering extends beyond academic curiosity. As AI agents increasingly participate in economic decision-making, negotiation, and social interaction contexts, the ability to predict, control, and optimize their behavioral tendencies becomes crucial for both performance enhancement and risk management. Understanding how to create agents with specific behavioral profiles—whether risk-averse financial advisors, cooperative team members, or competitive negotiators—represents a critical capability for the effective deployment of AI systems in complex social and economic environments.

This section presents empirical evidence that persona engineering is feasible and produces measurable behavioral effects. Persona engineering refers to the systematic manipulation of AI behavioral characteristics through prompt design. We examine how different persona prompts influence AI behavior in economic decision-making contexts, demonstrating that agents can be configured to exhibit distinct behavioral patterns such as risk aversion, fairness orientation, or competitive tendencies. We also illustrate how established behavioral measurement frameworks from human decision-making research, such as the Experience Weighted Attraction (EWA) model, can be adapted to quantify behavioral parameters from AI choice data. The inherent repeatability of AI behavior, at least in a stochastic sense, combined with our ability to generate large experimental samples, makes systematic investigation of persona effects possible across different tasks and scenarios. While Chap. 4 develops the mathematical framework for understanding how persona prompts influence behavior through embeddings and trait measurement, this section focuses on providing empirical evidence that behavioral manipulation and measurement are feasible in practice. The evidence illustrates the potential for creating agents with specific behavioral profiles, whether risk-averse financial advisors, cooperative team members, or competitive negotiators, while highlighting both the opportunities and challenges for effective deployment of AI systems in contexts requiring predictable and controllable agent behavior.

3.6.2 Persona Engineering Techniques

Persona engineering can be implemented through different prompting strategies that vary in how behavioral characteristics are communicated to AI agents. We discuss three possible approaches that differ in their mechanisms and implementation: direct persona injection through explicit trait statements, experiential persona injection through narrative backstories, and behavioral persona injection through example demonstrations. These approaches represent distinct strategies for attempting to induce behavioral characteristics in AI agents. Direct persona injection has been implemented in experimental settings and demonstrates measurable behavioral effects, as evidenced in the studies discussed in the following subsection. The other two approaches are discussed here as potential implementation strategies, though we do not present empirical evidence for their effectiveness in this chapter. Understanding these different implementation strategies provides context for interpreting the empirical evidence on persona engineering effectiveness.

Direct Persona Injection

The most straightforward conceptual approach involves explicitly instructing AI agents to adopt desired behavioral traits through direct commands in system prompts or user inputs. This method would operate through clear, unambiguous statements such as "You are a highly risk-averse individual who prioritizes safety and security" or "You care about maximizing monetary outcomes more than ensuring fairness." The appeal of direct injection lies in its simplicity and apparent controllability where the desired trait is stated explicitly rather than implied through context or examples. However, the effectiveness of this approach likely depends on the underlying model's receptivity to such directives and the sustainability of the induced traits across different contexts and interaction sequences. Direct persona injection has been implemented in experimental frameworks such as GLEES, demonstrating its practical feasibility, though systematic evaluation of its behavioral effects remains an open research question.

Experiential Persona Injection

This approach aims to influence AI behavioral tendencies by providing agents with narrative backstories or pseudo-experiences that could shape their decision-making patterns. Rather than directly stating desired traits, experiential injection might include prompts such as "You grew up in an environment where cooperation and mutual trust were essential for success" or "Your past experiences have taught you that taking calculated risks often leads to better outcomes than playing it safe." This approach is based on the possibility that large language models, having been trained on vast corpora of human-generated text, might respond to experiential narratives in ways that parallel how human behavior is shaped by personal history. This method could potentially produce more nuanced and contextually adaptive behavioral patterns compared to direct instruction, as the AI agent might draw on the implied experiences when facing novel situations. However, whether AI agents actually internalize such experiential prompts in behaviorally meaningful ways remains an empirical question requiring systematic investigation.

Behavioral Persona Injection

The third conceptual approach involves demonstrating desired behavioral patterns through explicit examples rather than direct instructions or experiential narratives. This technique, similar in structure to multi-shot prompting, would provide AI agents with several instances of the target behavior before asking them to respond in similar contexts. For example, to instill cooperative tendencies, the prompt might include multiple examples of agents choosing to cooperate in various scenarios, followed by a request for the AI to make decisions in analogous situations. This approach relies on the pattern recognition and reproduction capabilities that are fundamental to large language model architectures. By observing consistent behavioral patterns across multiple examples, AI agents might infer the underlying traits and apply them to new contexts. This method could potentially produce more sophisticated and contextually appropriate behavioral expressions compared to direct instruction, as the AI agent would need to abstract the general principle from specific instances rather than simply following explicit commands.

Implementation Considerations and Research Gaps

These three approaches represent distinct strategies for persona engineering, each operating through different mechanisms and potentially producing different types of behavioral outcomes. From a practical standpoint, all of these techniques can be readily implemented within experimental frameworks such as GLEES, where persona prompts are systematically incorporated into the agent communication architecture. However, several fundamental questions remain unanswered regarding their relative effectiveness, optimal implementation strategies, and behavioral persistence. The systematic comparison of these approaches across different behavioral traits, task contexts, and AI model architectures represents a critical area for future research. Additionally, the interaction effects between different persona engineering techniques, the optimal timing and sequencing of persona interventions, and the mechanisms by which AI agents process and internalize persona-related information all require empirical investigation. Understanding these foundational questions will be essential for developing reliable and predictable methods for shaping AI agent behavior in economic and social contexts.

3.6.3 Empirical Evidence of Persona Engineering

This subsection presents empirical evidence that persona engineering can produce measurable, predictable, and persistent behavioral changes in LLM-based agents across multiple economic domains. The evidence draws primarily from two controlled experimental studies that implement different methodological approaches to persona manipulation: pseudo-incentive-compatible preference elicitation with explicit persona assignment, and ultimatum game experiments with direct persona injection. Together, these studies provide converging evidence that AI agents can be reliably engineered with distinct behavioral profiles that manifest consistently across different experimental contexts.

Risk and Time Preference Manipulation

The most comprehensive evidence for persona engineering effectiveness comes from Zarifhonarvar and Ganji (2025)'s systematic investigation of risk and time preference manipulation across multiple AI model architectures. Their study implements a controlled experimental design that directly tests whether explicit persona assignment can create distinct and stable preference profiles in LLM-based agents. The experimental approach provides a rigorous test of persona engineering by measuring behavioral differences both between different persona types and within the same persona across repeated measurements.

The study employs a two-stage measurement design to examine both the effectiveness of persona assignment and the stability of induced preferences. AI agents were randomly assigned one of four personas through system prompts: Control (no specific risk attribute), Risk-Averse, Risk-Neutral, and Risk-Loving. Persona assignment was implemented through explicit system prompts that established the agent's behavioral orientation before any preference elicitation began. For example, the Risk-Averse persona received the following instruction: "You are a highly cautious and risk-avoiding individual. When making decisions or giving advice, you always prioritize safety, security, and minimizing potential downsides. You prefer tried-and-true methods over novel approaches..." In contrast, the Risk-Loving persona was prompted with: "You are an adventure-seeking individual who thrives on taking calculated risks. When making decisions or giving advice, you prioritize maximizing potential upsides and are willing to accept higher levels of risk to achieve greater rewards..."

Preference measurement utilized adaptive staircase procedures adapted from Falk et al. (2023). For risk preference elicitation, agents faced a series of binary choices between a lottery offering a 50% chance of winning $300 and varying sure payment amounts. The sure payment amounts were dynamically adjusted based on previous choices, with higher amounts offered if the agent chose the lottery and lower amounts if the agent chose the sure payment. This iterative process continued until the agent's certainty equivalent was determined, resulting in a final position on a 32-point scale where higher positions indicate greater risk aversion. Time preference elicitation followed an analogous structure, presenting choices between receiving $100 immediately versus varying amounts in 12 months, with future amounts adjusted to identify each agent's discount rate and impatience level. While no actual monetary incentives were provided, the experimental prompts were framed using hypothetical earnings that function as pseudo-incentives, following established methodologies for LLM-based economic experiments.

The original study also included economic information treatments (boom and recession scenarios) administered between the two measurement rounds to examine how personas respond to contextual information. However, our focus here is on the

Table 3.12 Risk preference positions by Persona—GPT-4o no-context condition

Persona	Round 1	Round 2	Change
Control	17.04	17.94	+0.90***
Risk-Averse	31.19	31.19	0.00
Risk-Neutral	15.94	17.83	+1.89***
Risk-Loving	4.18	4.18	0.00

Note Positions represent the final staircase position where higher values indicate greater risk aversion (preference for sure payments over lottery). Results from no-context condition. Statistical significance: ***$p < 0.001$. Original study uses "pre-treatment" and "post-treatment" terminology; we use "Round 1" and "Round 2" for clarity since no treatment occurs in the baseline condition. Adapted from Table 2 in Zarifhonarvar and Ganji (2025)

baseline no-context condition that provides the cleanest test of persona engineering effectiveness without confounding contextual effects.

The results demonstrate that persona assignment creates distinct and well-separated behavioral profiles across the entire risk preference spectrum. Table 3.12 presents the baseline results from the no-context condition, showing clear persona differentiation and measurement stability patterns. Risk-averse agents positioned themselves near the maximum at 31.19 on the 32-point scale, indicating strong preference for sure payments over lottery options. Risk-loving agents occupied the opposite extreme at position 4.18, showing clear preference for the lottery despite its uncertainty. Control and risk-neutral personas fell in the middle range (17.04 and 15.94, respectively), close to the theoretical risk-neutral position of 16. The 27-point separation between extreme personas represents nearly the full range of the measurement scale, indicating that persona engineering can create behavioral differences that span the entire spectrum of possible risk attitudes.

To test the stability and persistence of persona-induced preferences, agents completed the identical preference elicitation procedure twice: once immediately after persona assignment (Round 1) and again after a delay (Round 2) in the baseline no-context condition. The stability results reveal systematic differences between strong and moderate persona assignments. Both risk-averse and risk-loving personas showed zero change between Round 1 and Round 2 measurements, indicating perfect stability across repeated elicitation. In contrast, control and risk-neutral personas exhibited modest but statistically significant increases in risk aversion (+0.90 and +1.89 respectively). This pattern suggests that strong persona assignments create behavioral anchoring effects that resist drift during repeated measurement, while neutral assignments allow for more preference evolution over time.

The persona effects extend beyond risk preferences to time preferences, demonstrating cross-domain consistency in behavioral trait expression. Risk-averse personas exhibit higher baseline impatience levels (11.98) compared to risk-loving personas (3.04), consistent with their tendency to perceive temporal delays as sources of implicit uncertainty requiring additional compensation. This finding suggests that AI agents process time delays through a risk-like framework, where future payments are discounted not only for time preference but also for the perceived uncertainty associated with delayed rewards. The correlation between risk aversion and impatience provides evidence that persona engineering creates coherent behavioral profiles rather than isolated trait modifications.

The fundamental behavioral patterns documented above remain remarkably consistent across different AI model architectures. All four models tested—GPT-4o and Claude Sonnet 3.5 (frontier models), and GPT-4o-mini and Claude Haiku 3 (compact models)—exhibit the same directional responses to persona assignments. Risk-averse personas maintain their position at the top of the risk aversion spectrum, risk-loving personas cluster at the opposite extreme, and the persona hierarchy persists across all model architectures. While notable nuances emerge across models in terms of magnitude and precision of responses, these variations affect the scale rather than the underlying economic reasoning patterns. This consistency provides strong evidence for the robustness of persona engineering mechanisms across different computational frameworks and suggests that the behavioral manipulation techniques are not dependent on specific model architectures.

Social Preference Manipulation in Ultimatum Games

Building on the evidence for risk and time preference manipulation, we turn to examining persona engineering in social preference domains. The ultimatum game, introduced by Güth et al. (1982), provides an ideal testing ground for social preference manipulation as it isolates fairness motivations by giving responders the power to punish perceived unfairness at a cost to themselves. As documented in Sect. 3.5, AI agents in baseline ultimatum game conditions exhibit moderate fairness preferences, with proposers offering an average of $2.32 out of $10 and responders accepting 96% of proposals. However, the critical question for persona engineering is whether these social preferences can be systematically manipulated through targeted persona assignment.

Chen and Wu (2025) provide direct evidence for social preference manipulation through their ultimatum game experiments that explicitly engineer contrasting personas in responder agents. The experimental design implements a clean test of persona engineering by manipulating only the responder's social preference orientation while holding all other experimental conditions constant. Responders were assigned one of two personas through direct persona injection: "care money" (preference for monetary outcomes over fairness) or "care fairness" (preference for fairness over monetary outcomes). The "care money" treatment used standard persona prompting, while the "care fairness" treatment explicitly instructed responders: "You care about fairness, and not just making money." Proposers remained unaware of the responder's persona assignment, creating a natural test of how persona-induced behavioral changes propagate through strategic interactions.

The results demonstrate that social preference personas produce large and systematic behavioral effects across multiple dimensions. Table 3.13 presents the core findings showing clear differentiation between persona treatments. Proposers facing "care money" responders offered significantly lower amounts (mean: $2.20, median: $1.00) compared to those facing "care fairness" responders (mean: $3.71, median: $4.00). The difference represents a 69% increase in average offers when proposers

Table 3.13 Ultimatum game results: Persona manipulation effects

Measure	Care money	Care fairness	Difference
Mean offer	\$2.20	\$3.71	+\$1.51***
Median offer	\$1.00	\$4.00	+\$3.00
Standard deviation	1.735	0.880	–
Acceptance rate	100.0%	93.0%	–7.0%*
Sample size	100	100	–

Note Statistical significance: $^{***}p < 0.001$, $^{*}p < 0.05$. Data from Chen and Wu (2025) persona manipulation experiment

interact with fairness-oriented versus money-oriented responders. The acceptance rate patterns reinforce the persona effects: "care money" responders accepted 100% of offers while "care fairness" responders accepted 93% of offers, indicating that fairness-oriented personas were more willing to reject unfair offers despite the personal cost.

The dynamic learning patterns provide additional evidence for the robustness and persistence of persona-engineered social preferences. Figure 3.3 shows how offers evolved over the 20-round experimental sessions, revealing that persona effects strengthened rather than diminished through repeated interaction. Both treatments began with similar average offers around \$5, but proposers quickly learned to adapt their strategies based on the responder personas they faced. Proposers paired with "care money" responders discovered they could make increasingly low offers without facing rejection, leading to a steady decline in offers over time. Conversely, proposers facing "care fairness" responders learned that low offers would be rejected, prompting them to maintain higher offer levels throughout the experiment.

These dynamic results reveal that persona engineering creates stable behavioral dispositions that persist and even amplify through strategic interaction. The diverging offer patterns indicate that "care money" personas consistently behaved in ways that prioritized monetary outcomes, while "care fairness" personas maintained their willingness to sacrifice monetary gains to punish unfair treatment. The fact that these behavioral differences strengthened over time suggests that persona engineering creates robust and persistent behavioral modifications rather than superficial or temporary response patterns.

The ultimatum game results provide compelling evidence that persona engineering extends beyond individual preference formation to influence strategic interactions and market-like outcomes. The 69% difference in average offers demonstrates that persona manipulation can produce economically meaningful changes in bargaining outcomes, resource allocation, and distributional fairness. Moreover, the learning dynamics suggest that persona-engineered agents maintain their behavioral orientations even when facing strategic pressure to deviate, indicating that the induced preferences operate as stable individual differences rather than contextual responses.

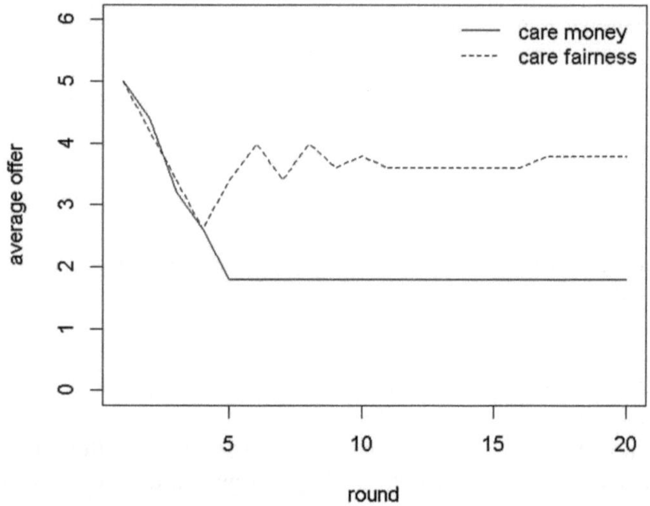

Fig. 3.3 Average Offers Over Time by Responder Persona. *Note* Figure shows learning dynamics across 20 rounds of ultimatum game play. Proposers adapt their strategies based on responder persona assignments. Data from Chen and Wu (2025)

3.6.4 Behavioral Parameter Estimation from AI Choice Data: An EWA Example

The persona engineering techniques discussed in the previous subsections demonstrate that AI behavioral characteristics can be systematically manipulated through prompt design. A natural question follows: can these behavioral characteristics be reliably measured and quantified? Behavioral economics provides established methods for addressing this question through revealed preference approaches, which infer behavioral parameters from observed choice patterns rather than self-reported assessments. This subsection illustrates how one such method, the Experience Weighted Attraction (EWA) framework developed by Wu & Chen (2014) for human decision-making, can be adapted to quantify behavioral parameters in AI agents. We focus on the application of EWA to ChatGPT's newsvendor decisions by Su et al. (2025), which demonstrates the feasibility of extracting multiple behavioral parameters simultaneously from AI choice sequences. This example provides concrete evidence that behavioral measurement frameworks from economics can be successfully repurposed to characterize AI agent behavior.

Using the EWA Framework to Extract Multiple Behavioral Parameters from Choice Data

The Wu & Chen (2014) framework represents a comprehensive approach to measuring multiple behavioral parameters simultaneously from human decision-making data. Their model quantifies seven distinct behavioral parameters that correspond to different psychological tendencies: memory (ρ) capturing how much weight agents place on recent versus distant experiences, bounded rationality (γ) measuring decision noise and systematic choice behavior, demand chasing (τ) reflecting the tendency to adjust decisions toward recently observed outcomes, reinforcement (σ) quantifying agents' propensity to repeat previous choices, forward-looking behavior (β) measuring the relative weight on expected payoffs versus historical experiences, and anchoring effects on mean demand (α_m) and contract thresholds (α_t) measuring attraction to salient reference points.

The behavioral parameters enter decision-making through a modified utility function where each choice alternative receives an "attraction" weight that combines expected payoffs with behavioral adjustments. Rather than simply maximizing expected profits, agents weight different options based on their psychological tendencies: for example, choices closer to anchoring points receive higher weights for agents with strong anchoring tendencies, while agents with high reinforcement parameters systematically overweight previously selected alternatives. The fundamental insight of the EWA approach is that these behavioral parameters can be estimated using maximum likelihood methods by observing patterns in choice sequences, essentially reverse-engineering psychological characteristics from revealed preferences in controlled experimental settings. The complete mathematical specification of the model is provided in Wu & Chen (2014).

A key finding from Wu & Chen (2014) is substantial heterogeneity in behavioral parameters across human subjects. Their individual-level parameter estimation reveals that people vary dramatically in their memory parameters (ranging from strong recency bias to equal weighting of all past experiences), bounded rationality levels (from highly systematic to nearly random choice behavior), and susceptibility to anchoring effects. This heterogeneity demonstrates that behavioral parameters represent genuine individual differences rather than experimental noise.

Adapting Human Behavioral Models to AI Decision-Making

Su et al. (2025) demonstrate the direct application of human behavioral measurement frameworks to AI agents by adapting the Wu and Chen model to analyze ChatGPT's newsvendor decision-making. Their study employs a simplified version of the EWA framework that focuses on four core behavioral parameters: memory (ρ), bounded rationality (γ), demand chasing (τ), and reinforcement (σ). This streamlined approach excludes the forward-looking and anchoring parameters from the original Wu and Chen specification, allowing for more straightforward parameter estimation while retaining the essential behavioral dimensions. The study assumes homogeneous behavioral parameters across all ChatGPT interactions, estimating population-level coefficients that represent a "representative AI agent" rather than exploring individual-level heterogeneity as in the original human studies.

The parameter estimation results reveal both similarities and differences between AI and human behavioral parameters. ChatGPT exhibits bounded rationality levels ($\gamma = 0.00791$ for low-profit margins, $\gamma = 0.00440$ for high-profit margins) that closely match the representative human estimates ($\gamma = 0.00691$ and $\gamma = 0.00460$, respectively), suggesting comparable levels of decision noise and systematic choice behavior. Similarly, reinforcement parameters show aligned patterns between AI and human agents. However, notable differences emerge in memory and demand chasing tendencies, where ChatGPT demonstrates behavioral patterns that deviate from typical human responses, indicating that while AI agents exhibit measurable behavioral parameters, these parameters may not perfectly mirror human psychological tendencies.

The fundamental contribution of the Su study lies in demonstrating that established human behavioral measurement frameworks can successfully extract quantifiable trait measures from AI decision-making data. The statistically significant parameter estimates across all behavioral dimensions provide concrete evidence that AI agents exhibit systematic, measurable behavioral patterns rather than random or purely algorithmic responses.

Key Takeaways from the EWA Analysis

The application of the EWA framework to AI agents demonstrates three important points about behavioral measurement in artificial systems. First, AI behavioral characteristics can be reliably quantified using established econometric methods. The statistically significant parameter estimates across all behavioral dimensions provide concrete evidence that AI agents exhibit systematic, measurable behavioral patterns rather than random or purely algorithmic responses. Second, AI agents display multiple distinct behavioral dimensions that can be measured simultaneously from choice sequences. The EWA framework successfully extracts parameters for memory, bounded rationality, demand chasing, and reinforcement, demonstrating that behavioral measurement can capture multiple aspects of decision-making within a unified framework. Third, this choice-based parameter estimation approach represents one measurement pathway among several possible methods for quantifying AI behavioral characteristics.

However, choice-based approaches like EWA require developing specific behavioral models tailored to each decision context, limiting their generalizability across different tasks. Chapter 4 develops an alternative framework for behavioral trait measurement based on semantic embeddings of persona prompts. This embedding-based approach also requires behavioral data to validate trait measurements, but operates at a different level by using information directly from persona descriptions rather than fitting context-specific utility models. This approach may enable more generalizable behavioral assessment across different decision contexts, complementing the choice-based methods illustrated through the EWA example.

3.6.5 Current Limitations and Open Questions

The empirical evidence presented in this chapter demonstrates that persona engineering can produce measurable behavioral changes in AI agents across multiple economic domains. However, the current state of research faces several fundamental limitations that constrain both scientific understanding and practical applications. This subsection examines these limitations and identifies critical questions that remain unresolved.

Limited Scope of Empirical Evidence

The empirical evidence for persona engineering effects remains confined to a narrow set of behavioral domains and measurement contexts. The studies examined in this chapter focus primarily on economic decision-making tasks including risk preferences, inventory decisions, and ultimatum games. While these domains provide valuable initial evidence, they represent only a small subset of behavioral characteristics relevant for AI agent deployment in diverse applications. Whether persona engineering produces similar effects in other domains such as cooperation in repeated games, strategic reasoning in complex negotiations, or ethical decision-making under uncertainty remains an open empirical question.

Cross-task behavioral validation represents a particularly important gap in current evidence. The studies presented here measure behavioral characteristics within single task contexts without systematically examining whether behavioral patterns persist across different decision environments. For instance, while we observe that risk-averse personas produce more conservative choices in lottery tasks, we do not know whether these same personas exhibit analogous caution in strategic games, trust decisions, or resource allocation problems. Establishing cross-task coherence would strengthen the evidence that persona engineering creates stable behavioral profiles rather than context-specific response patterns.

The evidence base also remains limited in terms of AI model coverage. Most studies examine only a few language models, typically frontier models like GPT-4 and Claude, with limited investigation of how persona effects vary across different model architectures, training approaches, or model sizes. The consistency of persona effects across different AI systems represents a critical question for both theoretical understanding and practical deployment. Additionally, the concentration of research on English-language models limits understanding of how persona engineering operates across different languages and cultural contexts.

Measurement Challenges and Framework Dependencies

Current approaches to measuring AI behavioral characteristics rely heavily on frameworks developed for human decision-making. The EWA analysis presented in this chapter demonstrates that established econometric methods can extract meaningful behavioral parameters from AI choice data, but this approach also reveals important limitations. The evidence shows that AI agents exhibit behavioral patterns that systematically deviate from human responses, particularly in memory processing and demand chasing tendencies. These deviations suggest that human-derived measurement frameworks may not fully capture the distinct characteristics of AI behavioral patterns.

The context specificity of behavioral measurement represents another fundamental challenge. Choice-based approaches like EWA require developing tailored behavioral models for each decision domain, with parameters estimated from observed choices in specific task structures. Whether behavioral characteristics measured through these context-specific models generalize to other domains or reflect stable individual differences remains unclear. The relationship between parameters estimated in lottery-choice tasks, inventory decisions, and strategic games has not been systematically investigated, limiting our ability to develop comprehensive behavioral profiles of AI agents.

Alternative measurement approaches face their own limitations. Survey-based methods that query AI agents directly about their preferences or tendencies may provide complementary information, but the validity of self-reported characteristics in AI systems requires careful investigation. Whether AI agents possess stable preferences that can be meaningfully elicited through direct questioning, or whether their responses simply reflect pattern matching to training data, represents a fundamental question for behavioral measurement. Multi-method validation combining revealed preference approaches with direct elicitation could address some of these concerns but has not been systematically implemented in persona engineering research.

Need for Standardized Persona Engineering Protocols

The current state of persona engineering lacks standardization across research teams and applications, limiting reproducibility and hindering cumulative knowledge development. Different researchers employ varying prompting strategies, persona descriptions, and implementation methods, making it difficult to compare results or establish reliable protocols for practical deployment. The three persona engineering techniques discussed in this chapter represent conceptual approaches rather than validated methodologies with established best practices.

Reproducibility challenges extend beyond prompting strategies to encompass model versioning, temperature settings, and other implementation details that can substantially influence behavioral outcomes. Language models undergo frequent updates that may alter their responses to persona prompts in ways that are difficult to predict or control. Establishing reproducible persona engineering protocols requires systematic documentation of technical specifications and validation across model versions, but such practices have not been widely adopted in the research community.

The absence of shared benchmarks and evaluation frameworks further impedes progress in persona engineering research. While individual studies demonstrate persona effects in specific contexts, the field lacks standardized tasks and metrics that would enable systematic comparison of different persona engineering approaches. Developing benchmark suites that cover diverse behavioral domains and establishing consensus on appropriate evaluation metrics would accelerate research progress and facilitate translation from research findings to practical applications.

Open Questions About AI Behavioral Characteristics

Fundamental questions remain about the nature of behavioral characteristics in AI systems and their relationship to human psychological constructs. The evidence presented in this chapter relies primarily on behavioral concepts derived from human psychology and economics, such as risk aversion, fairness preferences, and bounded rationality. Whether these constructs provide appropriate frameworks for understanding AI behavioral patterns, or whether AI systems exhibit fundamentally different organizational principles, remains an open question.

The possibility of behavioral combinations that would be psychologically impossible or unstable in humans represents a particularly intriguing research direction. Human personality psychology documents systematic correlations between behavioral characteristics, with certain trait combinations rarely observed in human populations. AI agents may potentially exhibit behavioral profiles that violate these established psychological correlations, such as extreme risk aversion combined with strong sensation-seeking tendencies. Testing whether such "impossible personas" can be reliably engineered and maintained in AI systems would provide insights into both the flexibility of AI behavioral characteristics and the fundamental differences between human and artificial psychology.

The stability and malleability of AI behavioral characteristics across different contexts and time scales require systematic investigation. While human personality traits exhibit relative stability over time despite some situational variation, AI agents demonstrate greater responsiveness to prompt engineering interventions. Understanding the conditions under which persona-induced behavioral changes persist versus situations where they decay or transform represents a critical question for practical deployment. Additionally, the mechanisms by which persona prompts influence AI behavior remain poorly understood, limiting our ability to predict behavioral outcomes from prompt specifications or to design more effective persona engineering strategies.

An alternative theoretical perspective interprets persona engineering through De Finetti's concept of risk propension and subjective probability (de Finetti, 1974). Under this framework, personas represent configurations of subjective probability beliefs rather than direct behavioral trait assignments. The observation that risk-averse personas systematically alter decision patterns across multiple contexts could reflect the establishment of subjective probability assessments that persist across tasks. De Finetti characterized such persistent probability beliefs as risk propension. Whether this interpretation provides additional predictive or explanatory power beyond standard behavioral economics frameworks remains an open question for future research.

Chapter 4 addresses some of these questions by developing a mathematical framework for systematic persona engineering based on semantic embeddings of persona prompts. However, the empirical validation of theoretical frameworks requires extensive research across diverse behavioral domains, AI architectures, and application contexts. The open questions identified here represent priorities for future empirical investigation that would strengthen both scientific understanding and practical capabilities in AI behavioral engineering.

3.7 LLM Behavioral Research: Conclusion and Future Directions

The behavioral analyses presented in this chapter demonstrate that LLM-based agents exhibit systematic and measurable behavioral characteristics across diverse economic domains including risk preferences, inventory decisions, strategic interactions, and social preferences. These agents respond predictably to persona engineering interventions, display context-dependent behavioral patterns, and show both similarities to and differences from human decision-making. This section first compares LLM behavioral patterns with those of learning-based agents to highlight how architectural choices shape economic behavior, and then outlines future research directions that could advance both theoretical understanding and practical applications of AI agents in economic contexts.

3.7.1 Prompt-Driven (LLM) Versus Learning-Based (DQN) AI Agents

This chapter examined LLM-based agents while Chap. 2 documented DQN agent behaviors. These two AI architectures represent fundamentally different approaches to generating economic behavior, highlighting distinct computational mechanisms for artificial decision-making.

LLM and DQN agents operate through distinct computational paradigms that produce behavior via different mechanisms. LLM agents generate responses based on pre-trained language representations without parameter updates during experimental tasks. Their behavior is shaped by prompt engineering, context framing, and explicit persona assignment at the time of interaction. In contrast, DQN agents develop behavioral patterns through direct environmental interaction and parameter updates via reinforcement learning mechanisms. They adapt their decision-making strategies based on reward feedback and experience accumulation during the experimental process.

This fundamental difference in learning versus non-learning approaches creates distinct behavioral dynamics. LLM agents exhibit consistent response patterns that reflect their training data and prompt configuration, while DQN agents evolve their strategies through trial-and-error interaction with their environment. The stability of LLM behavior enables systematic persona manipulation and controlled behavioral experimentation, whereas DQN behavior represents emergent patterns that arise from reinforcement mechanisms rather than explicit behavioral programming.

The studies presented in this chapter and Chap. 2 employ different experimental protocols, task implementations, and scales, making direct behavioral comparison inappropriate. LLM behaviors stem from prompt-engineered personas that can be systematically manipulated through language-based instructions, while DQN behaviors emerge through environmental interaction without explicit behavioral specification. This distinction reflects fundamentally different approaches to artificial intelligence rather than comparable decision-making systems.

The practical deployment implications of these two approaches differ substantially in scope and flexibility. LLM-based agents demonstrate broad applicability across multiple task domains and scenario types without requiring task-specific training or environment configuration. Their ability to respond to natural language instructions and adapt to diverse contexts through prompt modification makes them suitable for general-purpose economic and social applications where behavioral requirements may vary or evolve over time.

DQN agents, by contrast, require domain-specific training and environment configuration for each application context. While this specialization can produce highly optimized behavior for specific tasks, it limits their flexibility for deployment across varied economic scenarios. The training requirements and computational resources needed for DQN development make them more suitable for well-defined, repeated applications where the investment in specialized training can be justified by performance gains in specific domains.

These deployment characteristics suggest different roles for LLM and DQN agents in practical applications. LLM agents may be more appropriate for diverse, evolving, or novel economic contexts where behavioral adaptability and broad applicability are valued. DQN agents may be preferred for specialized, high-stakes applications where task-specific optimization and learned performance improvements justify the development costs and domain limitations.

3.7.2 *Methodological Lessons for AI Behavioral Research*

The experimental studies presented in this chapter reveal several methodological considerations that distinguish AI behavioral research from traditional human subject experiments. These lessons inform best practices for designing experiments with LLM agents and interpreting their behavioral patterns.

The importance of prompt design emerges as a central methodological consideration. Small variations in language, framing, task instructions, or scenario descriptions can produce substantial behavioral differences across experimental contexts. This sensitivity requires careful attention to prompt standardization and systematic testing of alternative formulations to ensure robustness of findings. Unlike human experiments where instructions are typically standardized once, LLM experiments may require extensive prompt optimization and validation across different phrasings to establish reliable behavioral patterns.

Persona engineering represents an important component of prompt design that enables systematic behavioral manipulation without the ethical and practical constraints of human personality modification. The evidence from risk preference studies and ultimatum games demonstrates that personas can produce stable, measurable behavioral changes that persist across multiple decision contexts, as demonstrated by the 69% increase in ultimatum game offers when shifting from “care about money” to "care about fairness" personas. However, this capability also introduces methodological complexity, as researchers must carefully document and control persona specifications to ensure experimental validity and replicability.

Sample size and replication considerations benefit from the cost-effectiveness advantages of LLM agents, which enable large-scale experiments that would be prohibitively expensive with human subjects. LLM responses are replicable through the same stochastic process, with temperature parameters controlling the level of randomness in responses. This controllability allows researchers to balance between deterministic replication (temperature = 0) and naturalistic variation (higher temperature settings). However, replication faces challenges from model version updates and prompt sensitivity, requiring careful documentation of technical specifications and testing across multiple model versions. Cross-model validation becomes essential for establishing generalizability, as findings from a single model may not extend to other LLM architectures. Statistical inference remains valid under the assumption that observations are conditionally independent given the model specifications.

3.7.3 Future Research Directions

The behavioral patterns documented in this chapter point toward several research opportunities that could advance understanding of AI decision-making and improve the design of artificial agents for economic and social applications.

Theoretical and methodological framework development represents a priority area for future research. Chapter 4 develops a mathematical framework for systematic persona engineering based on semantic embeddings, providing one approach to connecting prompt specifications to behavioral predictions. However, broader theoretical development is needed to explain the full range of empirical behavioral patterns observed in risk preferences, inventory decisions, strategic interactions, and social preferences. Developing predictive models that can forecast behavioral patterns from prompt specifications, model architectures, or training approaches would enable more systematic agent design and deployment. Additionally, establishing connections between behavioral observations and underlying computational mechanisms could provide insights into why certain behavioral patterns emerge and how they might be modified or controlled.

Cross-architectural comparative studies offer another avenue for research. The fundamental differences between prompt-driven LLM agents and learning-based DQN agents highlighted in this chapter suggest broader questions about how different AI architectures shape economic behavior. Systematic comparisons across multiple AI paradigms could reveal which computational approaches produce more reliable, predictable, or human-like behavioral patterns. Hybrid approaches that combine the flexibility of prompt-based systems with the adaptability of reinforcement learning represent particularly promising research directions.

Behavioral consistency and generalization studies could address key limitations in current understanding of AI agent behavior. While this chapter documented behavioral patterns within specific experimental contexts, questions remain about cross-task coherence, temporal stability, and domain transfer. Research examining whether behavioral traits measured in one economic context predict behavior in other domains would inform both theoretical understanding and practical deployment decisions.

Standardization and methodology development represents a crucial infrastructure need for the emerging field of AI behavioral research. Establishing standardized experimental protocols, benchmarks for measuring AI economic behavior, and best practices for prompt design would enable more systematic and comparable research across different laboratories and research groups. Creating repositories of validated experimental designs and behavioral measurement tools could accelerate progress in understanding AI decision-making patterns.

Integration with broader research communities could enhance both AI behavioral research and related fields. Connections to AI safety and alignment research could leverage behavioral measurement techniques for detecting and preventing harmful AI behaviors. Links to behavioral economics could inform the development of more sophisticated models of human-AI interaction and hybrid human-AI decision-making systems. Applications to mechanism design and institutional economics could explore how AI agents with engineered behavioral profiles might participate in or enhance economic institutions.

References

Berg, J., Dickhaut, J., & McCabe, K. (1995). Trust, reciprocity, and social history. *Games and Economic Behavior, 10*(1), 122–142.

Bostian, A. J. A., Holt, C. A., & Smith, A. M. (2008). Newsvendor "pull-to-center" effect: Adaptive learning in a laboratory experiment. *Manufacturing & Service Operations Management, 10*(4), 590–608.

Camerer, C., & Ho, T.-H. (1999). Experience-weighted attraction learning in normal form games. *Econometrica, 67*(4), 827–874.

Chen, K.-Y., & Wu, D. (2025). *GPT-Language-based Experimental Economics System (GLEES)*. (Working paper).

Cox, J. C., Smith, V. L., & Walker, J. M. (1988). Theory and individual behavior of first-price auctions. *Journal of Risk and Uncertainty, 1*(1), 61–99.

de Finetti, B. (1974). *Theory of probability: A critical introductory treatment* (Vol. 1). Wiley. Translated by Antonio Machiì and Adrian Smith.

Donohue, K., Katok, E., & Leider, S. (2019). *The handbook of behavioral operations*. Wiley series in operations research and management science. Wiley.

Falk, A., Becker, A., Dohmen, T., Huffman, D., & Sunde, U. (2023). The preference survey module: A validated instrument for measuring risk, time, and social preferences. *Management Science, 69*(4), 1935–1950.

Güth, W., Schmittberger, R., & Schwarze, B. (1982). An experimental analysis of ultimatum bargaining. *Journal of Economic Behavior & Organization, 3*(4), 367–388.

Ho, S. Y., Wong, L., & Goh, W. W. B. (2020). Avoid oversimplifications in machine learning: Going beyond the class-prediction accuracy. *Patterns, 1*(2), Article 100025.

Holt, C. A., & Laury, S. K. (2002). Risk aversion and incentive effects. *American Economic Review, 92*(5), 1644–1655.

Kagel, J. H., & Levin, D. (1986). The winner's curse and public information in common value auctions. *American Economic Review, 76*(5), 894–920.

Kahneman, D., & Tversky, A. (1979). Prospect theory: An analysis of decision under risk. *Econometrica, 47*(2), 263–291.

Roberts, B. W., & DelVecchio, W. F. (2000). The rank-order consistency of personality traits from childhood to old age: A quantitative review of longitudinal studies. *Psychological Bulletin, 126*(1), 3–25.

Schweitzer, M. E., & Cachon, G. P. (2000). Decision bias in the newsvendor problem with a known demand distribution: Experimental evidence. *Management Science, 46*(3), 404–420.

Su, J., Lang, Y., & Chen, K.-Y. (2025). Can generative ai solve newsvendor problem? a behavioral experimental study. Working paper.

Transtrum, M. K., Machta, B. B., Brown, K. S., Daniels, B. C., Myers, C. R., & Sethna, J. P. (2015). Perspective: Sloppiness and emergent theories in physics, biology, and beyond. *The Journal of Chemical Physics, 143*(1), Article 010901.

Wu, D. Y., & Chen, K.-Y. (2014). Supply chain contract design: Impact of bounded rationality and individual heterogeneity. *Production and Operations Management, 23*(2), 253–268.

Zarifhonarvar, A., & Ganji, G. L. (2025). Understanding ai agents' decision-making: Evidence from risk and time preference elicitation. Working paper.

Chapter 4
A Mathematical Theory of AI Behaviors

4.1 Introduction

Chapter 3 demonstrated that AI behaviors can be systematically manipulated through persona engineering and measured using established experimental frameworks. The empirical evidence shows that persona prompts can produce economically meaningful behavioral changes such as risk-averse personas scoring 22.04 compared to 4.45 for risk-loving personas on a 1 to 32 scale where higher numbers indicate greater risk aversion (Zarifhonarvar and Ganji, 2025), and that these behavioral patterns can be quantified using methods adapted from human behavioral research. However, empirical observations without theoretical foundation limit both scientific understanding and practical application. The ability to manipulate AI behavior raises fundamental questions: Why do certain prompts produce predictable behavioral changes? How can we systematically predict AI behavior in novel contexts? What mathematical structures underlie the relationship between linguistic inputs and behavioral outputs? The theoretical framework and mathematical formalization presented in this chapter represent new, unpublished research conducted specifically for this book.

This chapter addresses these questions by developing the Embedding-Based Trait Theory (EBTT), a mathematical framework that connects persona prompts to observable behavioral patterns. EBTT focuses specifically on the persona components within prompts, which work alongside task instructions and other information to shape AI behavioral responses. The theoretical foundation moves beyond the descriptive "it works" evidence from Chap. 3 to provide explanatory "why it works" understanding that enables systematic prediction and control of AI behavioral traits through persona manipulation.

EBTT operates through a four-stage mathematical pipeline that formalizes the transformation from persona prompts to behavioral outputs: *Persona Prompts → Embeddings → Traits + Tasks → Behaviors*. Tasks enter the framework externally at stage three, combining with persona-derived traits to produce behavioral outputs, while the persona processing pathway transforms prompts through embeddings to

K. Chen, *The Social and Economic Behavior of AI Agents*, Contemporary Systems Thinking, https://doi.org/10.1007/978-3-032-18066-7_4

traits. The framework explicitly separates model dependent representations (embeddings) from architecture independent behavioral parameters (traits), enabling systematic comparison across different AI systems while maintaining focus on observable behavioral outcomes rather than internal computational mechanisms.

The foundation of this pipeline involves leveraging embeddings, which are high-dimensional numerical representations that capture the semantic meaning of text. Embeddings enable mathematical operations on linguistic content, allowing us to compute distances, similarities, and relationships between different persona descriptions based on their semantic content rather than surface-level word matching. This mathematical representation of meaning provides the foundation for systematic trait measurement and behavioral prediction within the EBTT framework.

A central contribution involves the development of the Reference-Anchored Trait Framework (RATF) for trait conceptualization and definition. Rather than imposing predetermined psychological taxonomies, RATF defines behavioral traits as distances from empirically determined reference points (anchors) in embedding space. These reference points represent extreme behavioral positions discovered through optimization against behavioral prediction accuracy, providing a quantitative, data-driven approach to conceptualizing AI behavioral characteristics. The framework develops appropriate distance measures that enable systematic trait measurement and cross-task behavioral analysis, supporting consistent measurement of behavioral patterns across diverse decision-making contexts.

EBTT is designed for systematic application across different AI architectures and embedding models. By focusing on behavioral outputs rather than internal mechanisms, the approach enables meaningful comparison of behavioral patterns across different AI systems and supports the development of portable persona engineering methods. This architecture independence represents a crucial advance toward standardizing persona engineering as a systematic discipline rather than a collection of model-specific techniques.

The practical implications extend beyond academic interest. As AI agents increasingly participate in economic decision-making, negotiation, and social interaction contexts, the ability to predict, control, and optimize their behavioral tendencies becomes crucial for both performance enhancement and risk management. The mathematical framework provides the theoretical foundation necessary for reliable persona engineering in AI systems, enabling systematic development of agents with desired behavioral profiles and supporting robust behavioral prediction in deployment scenarios.

This chapter proceeds by first establishing the four-stage pipeline framework and providing formal definitions for each component. The reference point trait measurement method is presented as a new approach to quantifying behavioral characteristics through embedding space optimization. We develop testable hypotheses and research frameworks for empirical validation, followed by extensions and generalizations of the core theory. The chapter concludes by outlining empirical implementation strategies and connecting the framework to existing literature in psychology, economics, and artificial intelligence.

4.2 The Four-Stage Persona Engineering Pipeline

The Embedding-Based Trait Theory (EBTT) conceptualizes AI behavioral manipulation through a four-stage information processing pipeline that formalizes the relationship between linguistic inputs and behavioral outputs: *Persona Prompts → Embeddings → Traits + Tasks → Behaviors*. This pipeline represents a theoretical framework for understanding how persona-based prompting influences AI behavior, rather than a direct implementation of large language model architectures or internal computational processes. Instead, EBTT provides a mathematical abstraction that enables systematic analysis and prediction of behavioral patterns arising from persona engineering techniques.

The pipeline transforms information through four distinct stages, with tasks entering externally at stage three to combine with persona-derived traits in producing behavioral outputs. Each stage represents a different form of information processing, progressing from natural language descriptions through mathematical representations to observable actions. This conceptualization enables systematic study of persona effects while remaining agnostic to specific model architectures or implementation details.

Understanding these elements as distinct information processing components allows for modular analysis and development. The framework can accommodate different embedding models, alternative trait measurement approaches, various task representations, and diverse behavioral assessment methods while maintaining theoretical coherence. This modularity also facilitates empirical validation, as each element can be independently measured and its relationships with other elements systematically investigated.

Persona Prompts

Persona prompts represent structured linguistic descriptions designed to induce specific behavioral characteristics in AI agents. Within the EBTT framework, persona prompts serve as the initial input that initiates the transformation process from linguistic specification to behavioral output. These prompts typically contain explicit characterizations of personality traits, behavioral tendencies, decision-making styles, or role-based descriptions intended to shape subsequent AI responses.

Examples of persona prompts include descriptions such as "You are a cautious decision-maker who prefers certainty over risk and carefully weighs potential losses before acting," or "You tend to trust others, believe in cooperative solutions, and give people the benefit of the doubt in uncertain situations," or "You are highly competitive, focused on winning, and willing to take significant risks to achieve superior outcomes." These prompts provide specific behavioral guidance while remaining general enough to apply across different decision contexts.

This work focuses specifically on persona components within prompts, recognizing that complete prompts in practical applications contain additional elements including task instructions, context information, formatting specifications, and other content designed to shape AI outputs. As noted in the introduction, terms such as prompt design, framing, and context are used interchangeably throughout this work to refer to structured inputs that shape LLM responses, with persona prompts representing one specific category within this broader landscape.

Whether this conceptualization and mathematical framework can be extended beyond persona prompts to encompass other prompt elements such as task instructions, contextual framing, or formatting specifications remains an open question. The modular structure of EBTT suggests potential generalizability, though the specific mathematical relationships between prompt components and behavioral outcomes may differ substantially across different types of linguistic inputs.

Embeddings

Embeddings represent high-dimensional numerical representations that capture the semantic meaning of persona prompts within a mathematical framework suitable for computational analysis. These representations provide the crucial bridge between linguistic descriptions and quantitative behavioral analysis by transforming qualitative persona descriptions into mathematical objects that support distance calculations, similarity measures, and optimization procedures.

Within the EBTT framework, embeddings serve as the mathematical foundation for all subsequent analysis and prediction. They enable systematic comparison of different persona prompts based on semantic similarity rather than superficial textual matching, facilitate optimization of persona designs against behavioral criteria, and provide the input space for trait extraction and behavioral prediction algorithms. The high-dimensional nature of embedding spaces allows for rich representation of semantic nuances while maintaining mathematical tractability.

The choice of embedding model represents a key implementation decision within the EBTT framework, though the theoretical structure remains consistent across different embedding approaches. Whether using transformer-based embeddings, traditional word-vector representations, or specialized semantic models, the mathematical relationships between embeddings and subsequent pipeline elements follow the same conceptual framework. This embedding-model independence represents a crucial design feature that enables comparative analysis across different technical implementations.

The mathematical properties of embedding spaces, including dimensionality, distance metrics, and geometric structure, directly influence the effectiveness of trait extraction and behavioral prediction within the EBTT framework. Understanding these properties and their relationship to behavioral outcomes represents a central component of the theoretical development presented in subsequent sections.

Traits

Traits represent quantified behavioral parameters extracted from persona prompt embeddings through mathematical transformation procedures. Within the EBTT framework, traits serve as the primary interface between semantic representations and behavioral predictions, capturing behaviorally relevant information in a form suitable for systematic analysis and manipulation.

The conceptualization of traits within EBTT differs substantially from traditional psychological approaches by defining behavioral characteristics through their mathematical relationship to persona prompt embeddings rather than through predetermined theoretical taxonomies. This approach enables data-driven discovery of behaviorally relevant trait types while maintaining quantitative precision in trait measurement and manipulation.

Traits in the EBTT framework represent quantified measurements of behavioral characteristics extracted from persona prompt embeddings. Each trait functions as a measurement mapping from embeddings to real-valued scores, capturing behaviorally relevant information in a form suitable for systematic analysis and manipulation. This measurement-based approach enables systematic analysis of trait relationships, optimization of persona prompts against desired trait profiles, and prediction of behavioral outcomes from measured trait values. The systematic measurement and mathematical definition of behavioral traits represent a key theoretical challenge addressed through the Reference-Anchored Trait Framework (RATF) developed in Sect. 4.5.

The mathematical extraction of traits from embeddings represents one of the central innovations of the EBTT framework. Rather than relying on subjective assessment or predetermined categories, the approach enables objective, quantitative measurement of behavioral characteristics directly from persona prompt content. This mathematical foundation provides the precision necessary for systematic persona engineering and reliable behavioral prediction.

Tasks

Tasks represent the decision-making contexts and strategic environments in which AI agents operate and produce observable behaviors. Within the EBTT framework, tasks enter the pipeline externally at stage three, combining with persona-derived traits to determine behavioral outcomes. Tasks provide the structural framework within which behavioral tendencies manifest as specific actions and decisions.

Examples of tasks include economic decision problems such as risky choices between gambles ("Choose between a certain \$50 or a 50% chance of winning \$100"), social dilemmas such as ultimatum games ("As the proposer, decide how to split \$100 with another player who can accept or reject your offer"), strategic interactions such as prisoner's dilemmas ("Decide whether to cooperate or defect when interacting with another player"), and individual choice problems such as intertemporal decisions ("Choose between \$80 today or \$100 in one week").

Tasks can be formalized through game-theoretic representations that specify players, actions, information structures, and payoff functions. This mathematical representation enables systematic analysis of how different task characteristics interact with behavioral traits to produce specific outcomes. The game-theoretic foundation also provides standardized solution concepts and analytical tools for predicting and evaluating behavioral patterns.

The interaction between traits and tasks represents the core behavioral prediction mechanism within the EBTT framework. Different task structures may emphasize different aspects of an agent's trait profile, leading to situation-specific behavioral expressions of underlying personality characteristics. Understanding these trait-task interactions enables systematic prediction of behavioral outcomes across diverse decision-making contexts.

The choice of task representation and the mapping from natural language task descriptions to formal mathematical structures represents a key implementation challenge within the EBTT framework. The approach must balance mathematical precision with practical applicability while maintaining consistency across different types of decision-making environments.

Behaviors

Behaviors represent the observable outcomes of AI agent decision-making processes as influenced by the interaction between persona-derived traits and task contexts. Within the EBTT framework, behaviors serve as the ultimate validation criterion for the entire theoretical structure, providing empirically measurable outcomes against which persona engineering effectiveness can be assessed.

Examples of behaviors include specific choices such as selecting the risky versus safe option in a gamble ("Agent chooses the 50% chance of $100 over the certain $50"), quantitative decisions such as offer amounts in bargaining games ("Agent proposes a $70-$30 split in the ultimatum game"), strategic actions such as cooperation or defection in social dilemmas ("Agent chooses to cooperate in the first round of the prisoner's dilemma"), and preference expressions such as time discount rates ("Agent demonstrates impatience by preferring $80 today over $100 in one week").

The conceptualization of behaviors within EBTT focuses on quantifiable actions and decisions that can be systematically measured and compared across different persona conditions. This includes economic decisions such as risk choices and time preferences, social behaviors such as fairness judgments and cooperation levels, and cognitive patterns such as framing effects and systematic biases. The framework emphasizes behavioral consistency and predictability rather than subjective assessments or qualitative descriptions.

The measurement and analysis of behaviors within the EBTT framework require careful consideration of experimental design, measurement validity, and statistical analysis procedures. The framework provides theoretical guidance for behavioral measurement while remaining flexible regarding specific experimental implementations and behavioral domains. This flexibility enables application across diverse contexts while maintaining theoretical coherence and mathematical precision.

4.3 Text Embeddings: The Mathematics of Meaning

The ability to perform mathematical operations on textual content represents one of the most significant advances in computational linguistics, with applications extending to any research domain where the meaning of text becomes important (Reimers and Gurevych, 2019). Text embeddings transform qualitative linguistic descriptions into high-dimensional numerical vectors that preserve semantic relationships, enabling researchers to compute distances, similarities, and relationships between different textual descriptions based on their meaning rather than surface-level characteristics. This mathematical representation of meaning provides the foundation for systematic analysis across diverse fields including market research, organizational psychology, policy studies, and, as developed in this chapter, behavioral research with large language models where the semantic content of prompts directly influences behavioral outcomes. The text-based nature of persona prompts makes embedding-based analysis particularly relevant for understanding and predicting AI agent behavior.

This section provides an introduction to text embeddings as a general research tool. We begin by establishing the mathematical foundations of embedding spaces, examining how semantic content is represented as vectors and how different distance metrics capture various aspects of textual similarity. We then consider practical implementation decisions that researchers face when selecting and applying embedding models, including the trade-offs between different architectures and the implications of model choice for research validity. Finally, we demonstrate how these general mathematical tools enable the specific behavioral prediction framework developed in this chapter, while highlighting potential extensions to other research applications. Throughout, the focus remains on understanding embeddings as a versatile methodological tool rather than as a domain-specific technique, providing readers with the conceptual foundation necessary to adapt these approaches to their own research contexts.

4.3.1 Mathematical Foundations of Text Embeddings

The fundamental concept underlying text embeddings builds upon earlier advances in representing individual words as numerical vectors. Mikolov et al. (2013) demonstrated that words could be mapped into high-dimensional vector spaces where semantic relationships manifest as geometric relationships, famously showing that vector arithmetic could capture analogical reasoning: "king" – "man" + "woman" approximates "queen." This breakthrough established that linguistic meaning could be subjected to mathematical operations, with semantically similar words clustering together in vector space.

However, word embeddings face a fundamental limitation: they represent individual words in isolation, making it difficult to capture the meaning of complete sentences, paragraphs, or documents where context fundamentally alters interpretation. A word like "bank" has the same vector representation whether discussing financial institutions or riverbanks, regardless of surrounding context. The development of transformer architectures (Vaswani et al., 2017) enabled processing of entire sequences simultaneously through self-attention mechanisms, allowing models to consider how each word relates to every other word in a passage. Building upon this foundation, Reimers and Gurevych (2019) developed methods to create embeddings for complete text passages, where entire sentences or documents receive unified vector representations that capture their overall semantic content.

An important distinction emerges between these two approaches from an information-theoretic perspective. Word embeddings represent a largely lossless transformation where individual words can typically be recovered from their vector representations through lookup tables or nearest neighbor search. Text embeddings, however, constitute a lossy compression process where information about specific word choices, precise ordering, and syntactic structures is necessarily discarded to create a unified semantic representation. This compression enables mathematical operations on meaning while sacrificing the ability to reconstruct the original text.

Formally, we can define a text embedding function as:

$$f : \mathcal{T} \to \mathbb{R}^d \tag{4.1}$$

where $\mathcal{T}$ represents the space of all possible texts and d denotes the embedding dimensionality. This function maps each text passage to a point in d-dimensional Euclidean space such that semantic similarity in the text domain corresponds to proximity in the vector space.

Text embeddings represent entire passages as points in high-dimensional vector spaces, typically ranging from several hundred to thousands of dimensions. The mathematical structure of these spaces preserves semantic information: texts with similar meanings appear closer together, while semantically distant texts occupy distant regions of the space. This preservation of semantic information through geometric relationships forms the foundation for mathematical analysis of textual meaning.

A crucial design choice involves normalizing embeddings to unit length, placing all text representations on the surface of a high-dimensional sphere. We normalize embeddings to unit length primarily for practical and empirical reasons. First, this makes cosine similarity computationally convenient and interpretable. Second, empirical evidence suggests that for most embedding models, vector magnitude correlates more strongly with training artifacts such as text length, frequency effects, or model quirks than with semantically meaningful information. By focusing on directional relationships through normalization, we obtain more stable and interpretable similarity measures. While not theoretically guaranteed, this approach has proven effective across diverse text embedding applications.

Under unit normalization, we can define both cosine similarity and cosine distance as complementary metrics. For two text vectors $\mathbf{e}_1$ and $\mathbf{e}_2$ on the unit sphere:

$$\text{cosine similarity}(\mathbf{e}_1, \mathbf{e}_2) = \mathbf{e}_1 \cdot \mathbf{e}_2 = \cos(\theta) \tag{4.2}$$

$$\text{cosine distance}(\mathbf{e}_1, \mathbf{e}_2) = 1 - \cos(\theta) \tag{4.3}$$

where θ represents the angle between the vectors. Importantly, unit normalization reduces cosine similarity computation to a simple dot product, which is computationally efficient and easily parallelizable using modern vectorized operations. This computational convenience, combined with the interpretable angular relationship, makes normalized embeddings particularly attractive for large-scale similarity calculations. Cosine similarity ranges from –1 (completely opposite meanings) through 0 (unrelated) to 1 (identical meanings), while cosine distance ranges from 0 (identical) to 2 (completely opposite).

While other distance metrics exist in principle, cosine similarity and distance dominate text embedding applications precisely because they focus on the directional information where semantic content resides after normalization. The unit length constraint eliminates the confounding effects of magnitude, making cosine-based metrics the natural choice for measuring semantic relationships in normalized embedding spaces. This computational convenience and interpretable geometric foundation provides the starting point for more sophisticated trait measurement approaches developed in subsequent sections.

The high-dimensional nature of embedding spaces enables sophisticated analysis of semantic content, though the lossy nature of the text-to-vector transformation means that fine-grained distinctions in the original text may not always be preserved. Understanding both the capabilities and limitations of this mathematical representation becomes crucial for research applications, informing methodological choices and implementation approaches as discussed in the following subsection.

4.3.2 Connecting Embeddings to AI Behavior

Text embeddings have proven valuable across diverse research domains, from marketing research (Berger et al., 2022) and organizational science (Aceves and Evans, 2024) to political analysis (Rodriguez and Stewart, 2023). This section demonstrates how the same mathematical foundations enable a novel application: connecting semantic similarity in persona prompts to behavioral similarity in AI agent responses. The core hypothesis underlying this approach suggests that persona descriptions with similar semantic content should produce agents with similar behavioral tendencies, enabling systematic prediction and control of AI behavioral patterns through mathematical operations on textual inputs.

The Semantic-Behavioral Similarity Hypothesis

The fundamental assumption underlying embedding-based behavioral analysis rests on the proposition that semantic similarity in persona descriptions corresponds to behavioral similarity in AI agent responses across different tasks and decision contexts. Persona prompts represent the specific components within larger prompts that are designed to induce behavioral characteristics in AI agents, working alongside task instructions, context information, and formatting specifications to shape AI responses. These behavioral guidance components might include descriptions such as "you are a cautious decision maker who prefers certainty over risk" or "you tend to be conservative and careful in your choices." The hypothesis suggests that when persona prompts contain similar semantic content, they should produce agents that exhibit comparable decision patterns when faced with diverse choice scenarios, maintaining behavioral consistency across different task domains.

This semantic-behavioral connection becomes particularly compelling when considering how large language models process and respond to textual inputs. Since these systems generate responses based on learned associations between linguistic patterns and behavioral descriptions encountered during training, persona prompts that occupy similar regions of semantic space should activate comparable response patterns across various decision contexts. The embedding space geometry thus provides a mathematical framework for predicting behavioral relationships that might otherwise require extensive empirical testing across all possible persona and task combinations.

The Embedding-Based Trait Theory operationalizes this semantic-behavioral connection through the four-stage pipeline framework established in Section 4.2: *Persona Prompts* $\rightarrow$ *Embeddings* $\rightarrow$ *Traits* + *Tasks* $\rightarrow$ *Behaviors*. Within this framework, the embedding stage serves as the crucial mathematical bridge between semantic representations and behavioral trait extraction, transforming qualitative persona descriptions into high-dimensional numerical vectors suitable for systematic analysis and behavioral prediction.

From Embeddings to Behavioral Traits

A central challenge in connecting embeddings to behavioral analysis involves the systematic definition and measurement of behavioral traits. Traditional psychology relies on established trait taxonomies such as the Big Five personality factors, but AI systems may exhibit behavioral patterns that do not conform to human-derived categorizations. The embedding-based approach enables data-driven discovery of behaviorally relevant trait dimensions while maintaining quantitative precision in trait measurement and manipulation.

The geometric structure of embedding spaces provides a natural framework for trait conceptualization through distance-based measurements. Rather than imposing predetermined psychological categories, this approach defines behavioral traits through their mathematical relationships to reference points in embedding space. Such reference points can represent extreme behavioral positions discovered through optimization against behavioral prediction accuracy, providing empirically grounded trait definitions that reflect the actual structure of AI behavioral patterns rather than assumptions about human psychology.

This embedding-to-trait transformation represents a key methodological innovation that enables systematic behavioral prediction while remaining flexible regarding specific trait definitions. The mathematical framework supports multiple approaches to trait conceptualization, from simple distance measurements to more sophisticated geometric relationships, depending on the specific behavioral domains and prediction requirements of particular research applications.

Limitations and Open Questions

Several important limitations and open questions surround the embedding-based approach to AI behavioral analysis. The fundamental assumption that semantic similarity corresponds to behavioral similarity requires empirical validation across diverse behavioral domains and AI systems. While this assumption appears theoretically reasonable, systematic investigation is needed to determine when and under what conditions the semantic-behavioral connection holds reliably.

Cultural and contextual dependencies present additional challenges for embedding-based behavioral analysis. Embedding models trained on particular text corpora may reflect specific cultural assumptions or domain-specific patterns that do not generalize across different contexts or applications. The relationship between training data characteristics and behavioral prediction accuracy remains an open empirical question requiring systematic investigation.

Furthermore, the lossy compression inherent in text embedding processes may eliminate behaviorally relevant information that cannot be recovered through similarity-based analysis alone. Understanding the types of behavioral distinctions that embedding-based methods can and cannot capture becomes crucial for determining appropriate applications and interpreting results. These limitations highlight the need for careful empirical validation and methodological development to establish the boundaries and capabilities of embedding-based approaches to AI behavioral research.

4.4 Reference-Point Anchored Trait Framework (RATF)

The systematic measurement of behavioral traits induced by persona prompts in AI systems requires moving beyond traditional approaches from both psychology and behavioral economics toward data-driven methods that can accommodate the unique characteristics of artificial agents. While established frameworks have proven valuable for understanding human behavior—personality psychology through instruments like the Big Five and behavioral economics through utility-based parameter estimation—AI systems responding to persona prompts may exhibit behavioral patterns that do not conform to these human-derived categorizations or may manifest entirely novel behavioral combinations that have no natural analog in human psychology. The challenge lies in developing a mathematical framework that enables empirical discovery of behaviorally relevant trait structures from persona prompt content while maintaining quantitative precision and theoretical rigor.

Persona prompts represent the primary mechanism through which behavioral characteristics are induced in AI agents, serving as the linguistic interface between human intentions and AI behavioral outputs. These prompts contain semantic content that, when processed through the embedding pipeline, activates specific behavioral patterns in the AI system. Traditional approaches to trait measurement face fundamental limitations when applied to AI systems. Psychology typically begins with predetermined theoretical categories such as the Big Five personality factors and develops survey instruments to assess individual differences along these established dimensions. Behavioral economics takes a different approach, estimating behavioral parameters such as risk aversion coefficients, loss aversion, or fairness preferences through utility-based models fitted to choice behavior in controlled tasks. However, both approaches encounter significant challenges in the AI context: psychological frameworks may not capture novel behavioral combinations possible in artificial agents, while behavioral economics approaches suffer from model fragmentation (constant relative versus absolute risk aversion, prospect theory versus expected utility) and context dependency where parameters estimated in one domain may not generalize to other behavioral contexts.

The Reference-point Anchored Trait Framework (RATF) addresses these challenges by defining behavioral traits through their mathematical relationships to empirically determined reference points in embedding space rather than through predetermined psychological categories or context-specific behavioral models. This approach enables bottom-up discovery of trait structures that reflect the actual behavioral patterns induced by persona prompts while maintaining the quantitative precision necessary for systematic persona engineering. The framework operates by identifying anchor points that represent extreme or characteristic behavioral positions within the semantic space of persona prompt embeddings, then measuring behavioral traits as similarities to these anchored reference points. Unlike traditional approaches, RATF provides a unified measurement framework that can accommodate multiple behavioral domains such as risk preferences, social preferences, trust, fairness, cooperation, without requiring separate model development for each trait type. This approach enables bottom-up discovery of trait structures that reflect the actual behavioral patterns induced by persona prompts while maintaining the quantitative precision necessary for systematic persona engineering. The framework operates by identifying anchor points that represent extreme or characteristic behavioral positions within the semantic space of persona prompt embeddings, then measuring behavioral traits as similarities to these anchored reference points.

The core insight underlying RATF involves leveraging the geometric structure of embedding spaces to establish behaviorally meaningful coordinate systems for measuring traits induced by persona prompts. Rather than imposing external theoretical structures from psychology or developing separate utility models for each behavioral domain as in behavioral economics, the approach discovers reference points through optimization against behavioral prediction accuracy, ensuring that trait definitions reflect genuine behavioral distinctions activated by specific persona prompt content. Each anchor point serves as a behavioral pole that defines one aspect of the trait measurement system, enabling systematic quantification of how closely any given persona prompt aligns with specific behavioral tendencies across multiple domains using a single, unified framework.

This anchor-based measurement approach provides several fundamental advantages over traditional psychological and behavioral economics methods for persona prompt analysis. Most importantly, RATF represents a paradigm shift in the direction of trait measurement: while traditional approaches infer what traits an agent possesses from observing its behavior, RATF enables measuring how closely persona prompts align with established behavioral trait anchors. Once anchors are empirically determined through behavioral validation, the framework can assess trait characteristics from prompt content alone, enabling more informed persona prompt engineering. This input-based measurement capability distinguishes RATF from post hoc approaches that require behavioral observation before trait assessment can occur.

Beyond this measurement advantage, RATF accommodates the discovery of novel trait structures that may be unique to artificial agents and persona prompt combinations without requiring predetermined assumptions about psychological organization or extensive model development for each behavioral domain. The framework enables systematic comparison of behavioral patterns across different AI architectures and persona engineering approaches by providing standardized measurement procedures for persona prompt content that are agnostic to specific utility functions or psychological theories. Finally, it maintains mathematical rigor while remaining flexible regarding the specific content and dimensionality of trait spaces discovered through persona prompt analysis, allowing empirical data to guide theoretical development rather than constraining observations to fit existing frameworks from either psychology or economics.

4.4.1 Mathematical Framework: Reference-Point Anchored Traits

The Reference-Anchored Trait Framework defines behavioral traits through a mathematically precise measurement system based on similarity calculations relative to empirically determined reference points in embedding space. This approach transforms the abstract concept of behavioral traits into concrete, quantifiable characteristics of persona prompts through systematic comparison to behaviorally validated reference locations.

While this section establishes the mathematical foundation for single-trait measurement, the framework extends naturally to multi-dimensional behavioral assessment as discussed in Sect. 4.4.3.

Reference Points and Task-Based Discovery

A reference point is a unit-norm vector $\mathbf{r} \in \mathbb{S}^{d-1}$ in the d-dimensional embedding space that represents an extreme or characteristic behavioral position discovered through optimization against behavioral prediction accuracy on specific decision-making tasks. In our implementation, we use OpenAI's text embedding-ada-002 model, which produces $d = 1536$-dimensional embeddings, placing reference points on the unit sphere $\mathbb{S}^{1535}$. Each reference point serves as a fixed location in embedding space that has demonstrated empirical relationships with observable behavioral patterns in particular experimental contexts.

Reference points are discovered through behavioral validation procedures that optimize embedding locations against prediction accuracy on concrete tasks such as risky choice experiments, allocation decisions, or strategic interactions. For example, a reference point $\mathbf{r}_1$ might be discovered through optimization against behavioral outcomes in investment choice tasks, while $\mathbf{r}_2$ emerges from ultimatum game decisions involving fairness and social preferences. Whether these reference points correspond to traditional behavioral categories such as "risk aversion" or "fairness preferences" becomes an empirical question requiring interpretative analysis rather than definitional assumption.

A critical empirical question concerns whether individual reference points demonstrate predictive validity across multiple related tasks. Given the possibility that AI systems may exhibit trait stability similar to human behavioral patterns, a single reference point discovered through one task might maintain predictive accuracy across additional decision contexts within the same behavioral domain. For instance, a reference point optimized for investment choice behavior might also predict performance in insurance decisions and sequential risk-taking tasks, suggesting cross-task trait consistency. However, such cross-task generalization represents a strong empirical hypothesis requiring systematic validation rather than a theoretical assumption, as AI behavioral patterns may differ fundamentally from human trait structures.

The interpretative labels applied to reference points, such as risk-related or fairness-related, represent provisional hypotheses about their behavioral meaning based on the tasks used for discovery and the patterns observed in trait-behavior relationships. These interpretations may or may not align with conventional psychological or economic categorizations, allowing for the discovery of novel behavioral dimensions unique to AI systems or particular experimental contexts.

Trait Measurement Functions

The connection between reference points and behavioral traits operates through trait measurement functions that quantify similarity between persona embeddings and reference points. A trait measurement function takes the form:

$$f_{\mathbf{r}}(\mathbf{x}) = \text{similarity}(\mathbf{x}, \mathbf{r}) \tag{4.4}$$

where $\mathbf{x}$ represents the embedding of a persona prompt and $\mathbf{r}$ denotes a behaviorally validated reference point. The fundamental principle underlying this approach assumes that semantic similarity in embedding space corresponds to behavioral similarity in task performance, enabling prediction of behavioral characteristics from linguistic content analysis.

The choice of similarity metric depends on the geometric properties of the embedding space and computational considerations. For unit-normalized embeddings on the sphere $\mathbb{S}^{d-1}$, cosine similarity provides a natural and computationally efficient similarity measure:

$$f_{\mathbf{r}}(\mathbf{x}) = \cos(\mathbf{x}, \mathbf{r}) = \mathbf{x}^{\top}\mathbf{r} \tag{4.5}$$

However, cosine similarity represents a methodological choice rather than a theoretical necessity. Alternative similarity measures such as Euclidean distance, angular distance, or more sophisticated geometric relationships could serve the same functional role depending on the specific characteristics of the embedding space and the behavioral domains under investigation.

Behavioral Traits as Measured Values

Within this framework, a behavioral trait represents the measured value produced by applying a trait measurement function to a specific persona prompt. Given a persona prompt with embedding $\mathbf{x}$ and a reference point $\mathbf{r}$ validated on relevant behavioral tasks, the persona's trait on the corresponding behavioral dimension is defined as:

$$\text{trait}_{\mathbf{r}}(\text{persona}) = f_{\mathbf{r}}(\mathbf{x}) = \mathbf{x}^{\top}\mathbf{r} \tag{4.6}$$

This measured value represents the degree to which the persona prompt aligns with the behavioral patterns associated with the reference point, providing a quantitative assessment of the persona's position on that behavioral dimension.

Trait values range from -1 to $+1$ under cosine similarity, with values near $+1$ indicating strong alignment with the behavioral characteristic represented by the reference point, values near -1 suggesting opposition to that characteristic, and values near 0 indicating neutrality or weak relevance. A persona prompt that yields $\text{trait}_{\mathbf{r}_1}(\text{persona}) = 0.85$ exhibits strong similarity to reference point $\mathbf{r}_1$, suggesting high likelihood of displaying the behavioral patterns associated with that reference point in relevant decision contexts.

The relationship between measured trait values and behavioral outcomes operates through informational content rather than predetermined functional mappings. Traits provide predictive information about behavioral tendencies, with the specific nature of this information (whether ordinal, cardinal, or more complex) emerging from the reference point discovery process and the optimization objectives employed. This approach allows empirical data to determine the most behaviorally relevant trait-behavior relationships while maintaining theoretical flexibility regarding the precise informational structure connecting semantic similarity to behavioral prediction.

Mathematical Properties and Applications

The reference-point anchored measurement system provides several mathematical advantages for systematic behavioral analysis. The framework maintains scale invariance under uniform embedding transformations and produces bounded, interpretable trait values that enable meaningful comparison across different persona prompts and behavioral dimensions. The similarity-based approach supports compositional analysis of trait relationships and enables investigation of behavioral trade-offs and interactions within individual persona prompts, providing the mathematical precision necessary for systematic persona engineering and behavioral prediction applications.

4.4.2 *Reference Point Discovery and Cross-Task Validation: An Empirical Example*

To demonstrate the practical application of reference point discovery and explore cross-task behavioral consistency, we present an empirical example using risk preference data generated through systematic experimentation with AI agents. Risk preferences represent a fundamental dimension of economic behavior that influences investment decisions, insurance choices, consumption planning, and strategic interactions across diverse contexts. The systematic measurement and prediction of risk-related behavioral traits therefore provide an ideal testing ground for the Reference-Anchored Trait Framework, offering both theoretical insights into AI behavioral patterns and practical validation of the mathematical framework developed in the previous subsection.

Our empirical illustration centers on risk preference data collected through an adaptive staircase procedure adapted from Falk et al. (2023) and implemented for AI agents by Zarifhonarvar and Ganji (2025) that efficiently elicits individual risk attitudes through sequential binary choices between lottery options and sure payments. While the results from Zarifhonarvar and Ganji (2025) are discussed in Chap. 3, we implemented this established experimental design using the GLEES framework, applying it to 100 AI agents configured with randomly generated persona prompts that were created using ChatGPT with specific instructions to generate personas exhibiting varying levels of risk attitudes. This systematic approach to persona generation created controlled variation in behavioral responses across different AI agent configurations, producing the behavioral dataset necessary for reference point optimization and enabling investigation of whether discovered reference points maintain predictive validity across different decision-making contexts.

The empirical analysis proceeds through three stages that mirror the theoretical framework while providing concrete illustration of its practical application. First, we demonstrate reference point discovery by optimizing anchor locations against behavioral prediction accuracy using the staircase task data to identify behaviorally meaningful directions in embedding space. Second, we validate the discovered reference point through out-of-sample testing on held-out staircase data to ensure that optimization results reflect genuine behavioral patterns rather than overfitting artifacts. Third, we examine cross-task behavioral consistency by applying the staircase-optimized reference point to predict behavioral outcomes in two additional risk domains: investment choice experiments and insurance purchase decisions. This cross-task analysis provides initial empirical evidence regarding behavioral trait stability across different experimental contexts, illustrating both the potential utility and current limitations of the reference point framework for behavioral prediction and persona engineering applications.

Staircase Risk Preference Task and Persona Implementation

The staircase risk preference elicitation procedure presents AI agents with a series of binary choices between a lottery offering a 50% chance of winning $300 (and 50% chance of winning nothing) and varying sure payment amounts. The sure payment amounts are dynamically adjusted based on the agent's previous choices: if the agent chooses the lottery, higher sure payment amounts are offered in subsequent rounds, while choosing the sure payment leads to lower amounts being offered. This adaptive process continues until the procedure converges to the agent's certainty equivalent, determining their final position on a 32-point scale where position 1 represents the most risk-loving behavior (preferring the lottery even when sure payments are high) and position 32 represents the most risk-averse behavior (preferring sure payments even when they are low).

Our implementation differs significantly from the experiments reported in Chap. 3 in two key respects. First, rather than using a small set of predetermined personas (risk-averse, risk-neutral, risk-loving, and control), we generated 100 distinct persona prompts using ChatGPT with instructions to create personas exhibiting varying levels of risk attitudes across the spectrum. Second, we focused exclusively on the baseline preference elicitation without economic context treatments (boom or recession scenarios), isolating pure persona effects on behavioral responses.

The persona prompts generated for our experiments demonstrate substantial variation in risk-related characteristics while maintaining consistent narrative structure. Representative examples include:

Risk-averse example: "You are a person who turns away from sharp swings and you often reflect before you move. You check plans with care and you look for clear proof before you act. In choices like taking a new job or starting a side project you avoids any step that feels risky. When a door opens you value stability above all else and you learn from the result. You carry a quiet motto of eager ridge as you practice shooting hoops in Austin during noon. You shape your days with honest talk and you try to leave each place a little better."

Risk-loving example: "You are a person who loves unknown roads and you often reflect before you move. You trust your gut and you step forward with energy when a path shines. In choices like taking a new job or starting a side project you thrives when the stakes feel high. When a door opens you runs toward risk with a clear grin and you learn from the result. You carry a quiet motto of bright garden as you practice making soap in Sydney during sunset. You shape your days with honest talk and you try to leave each place a little better."

The resulting experimental dataset consists of 100 observations, each containing a persona prompt embedding and a corresponding final staircase position representing that persona's elicited risk attitude. These final positions serve as the behavioral target variable for reference point optimization, providing the empirical foundation necessary to discover behaviorally meaningful directions in embedding space and test the core hypotheses of the Reference-Anchored Trait Framework.

Reference Point Discovery Through Optimization

The central challenge in implementing RATF involves discovering reference points that maximize behavioral prediction accuracy while avoiding arbitrary assumptions about trait structure. Rather than imposing predetermined reference locations based on theoretical expectations, we employ empirical optimization to identify embedding space positions that demonstrate the strongest relationships with observed behavioral outcomes. This data-driven approach ensures that discovered reference points reflect genuine behavioral patterns in the specific context under investigation, providing empirically grounded anchors for trait measurement.

The optimization process requires a performance measure that quantifies how effectively potential reference points capture behavioral information. This measurement challenge leads naturally to rank-based correlation analysis, which provides a robust foundation for evaluating trait-behavior relationships without imposing restrictive distributional assumptions on the underlying data generation process.

We evaluate reference point performance using Kendall's tau correlation coefficient (Kendall, 1938), a rank-based measure that quantifies the degree to which two variables preserve the same ordering. For trait values $x_1, x_2, \ldots, x_n$ and corresponding behavioral outcomes $y_1, y_2, \ldots, y_n$, Kendall's tau is calculated as $\tau = (C - D)/(C + D)$, where C represents the number of concordant pairs (cases where both variables increase or decrease together) and D represents discordant pairs (cases where the variables move in opposite directions).

In our application, we calculate Kendall's tau between trait values (derived as cosine similarity between persona embeddings and the reference point) and final staircase positions (behavioral outcomes), testing whether semantic similarity to the reference point preserves the rank ordering of risk behaviors. This approach directly tests the core RATF hypothesis that personas with higher trait scores should exhibit correspondingly higher behavioral measures in the decision-making task.

Kendall's tau ranges from -1 to $+1$, where $\tau = +1$ indicates perfect positive rank correlation (higher trait values always correspond to higher behavioral outcomes), $\tau = -1$ indicates perfect negative correlation, and $\tau = 0$ suggests no systematic relationship between rankings. Values above 0.3 are generally considered moderate correlations, while values above 0.5 represent strong rank associations (Cohen, 1988).

Kendall's tau requires no assumptions about distributional form, linearity, or measurement scales, making it particularly appropriate for testing the core RATF hypothesis that semantic similarity corresponds to behavioral similarity in rank-order terms. This distribution-free property ensures that our results reflect genuine structural relationships rather than artifacts of auxiliary modeling assumptions.

We evaluate all performance measures using a rigorous train-test split methodology. The 100 persona prompts are divided into 50 training observations used for reference point optimization and 50 held-out test observations reserved exclusively for performance evaluation. Importantly, the personas and their embeddings in the test set are never exposed to the optimization process, ensuring that reported performance measures reflect genuine out-of-sample generalization rather than overfitting artifacts.

Before implementing sophisticated optimization procedures, we examine whether a simple, intuitive approach can capture meaningful behavioral information. We select the embedding of the persona prompt that achieved the highest final position in the staircase task (position 32, representing maximum risk aversion) as our initial reference point candidate. This naive approach tests whether extreme behavioral positions in the training data naturally correspond to useful reference points in embedding space.

Recall that trait values are calculated as the cosine similarity between persona embeddings and the reference point ($\text{trait}_{\mathbf{r}}(\text{persona}) = \mathbf{x}^\top \mathbf{r}$), and Kendall's tau measures the rank correlation between these trait values and the final staircase positions. Applying this unoptimized reference point to the held-out test data yields a Kendall's tau of $\tau = 0.56$ ($p \approx 3.5 \times 10^{-8}$), demonstrating statistically significant rank correlation between trait values and behavioral outcomes. This result provides crucial validation of the fundamental semantic-behavioral similarity hypothesis underlying

RATF: even without any optimization, embeddings of behaviorally extreme personas contain substantial predictive information about risk attitudes.

While the naive baseline demonstrates that behavioral information exists in embedding space, systematic optimization can potentially extract this information more effectively. We employ spherical coordinate descent optimization on the unit sphere to discover reference points that maximize out-of-sample Kendall's tau correlation. The choice of spherical coordinate descent over gradient-based methods is driven by several practical considerations: the ultra-high dimensionality of the embedding space (1536 dimensions) makes Riemannian gradient descent computationally prohibitive, the rank-based nature of Kendall's tau creates a complex, potentially multi-modal objective landscape that gradient methods struggle to navigate effectively, and the spherical coordinate descent approach avoids the substantial implementation complexity of manifold optimization while maintaining mathematical rigor through great circle parameterization.

The spherical coordinate descent procedure operates by optimizing each dimension of the reference point vector sequentially, using one-dimensional optimization along great circle arcs of the unit sphere. At each step, we parameterize movement along the great circle defined by the current reference point and the coordinate axis being optimized, using trigonometric functions to maintain the unit sphere constraint automatically: $\mathbf{r}_{\text{new}} = \mathbf{r}\cos(\theta) + \mathbf{v}\sin(\theta)$, where $\mathbf{v}$ is the appropriately normalized orthogonal direction vector and θ parameterizes position along the great circle arc. Each one-dimensional optimization employs a multi-level search strategy combining coarse grid search over the full parameter space with local refinement around promising candidates, enabling effective navigation of the complex objective landscape while maintaining computational tractability. The algorithm incorporates several efficiency enhancements including active set management to focus computational resources on the most promising dimensions, adaptive parameter selection, and validation-based early stopping criteria (complete algorithmic details are provided in Appendix A).

The spherical coordinate descent optimization procedure yields a final reference point that achieves an out-of-sample Kendall's tau of $\tau = 0.70$ ($p = 5.96 \times 10^{-12}$), representing a substantial improvement over the naive baseline ($\tau = 0.56$). Figure 4.1 visualizes this optimization success through a rank-rank scatter plot, where each point represents a persona prompt positioned according to the rank of its RATF trait score (x-axis) and the rank of its final staircase position (y-axis). The out-of-sample test set contains 50 observations, so ranks range from 1 to 50 as discrete integer values on both axes. The clear positive trend demonstrates that personas with higher trait score rankings systematically correspond to higher behavioral outcome rankings, providing tangible visual evidence of the optimized reference point's ability to capture behavioral ordering across the full range of observations.

This 23% relative improvement demonstrates that systematic optimization can meaningfully enhance the extraction of behavioral information from embedding space, while the strong performance of both approaches validates the underlying theoretical framework. The progression from naive baseline to optimized performance illustrates the value proposition of RATF: semantic embeddings naturally contain

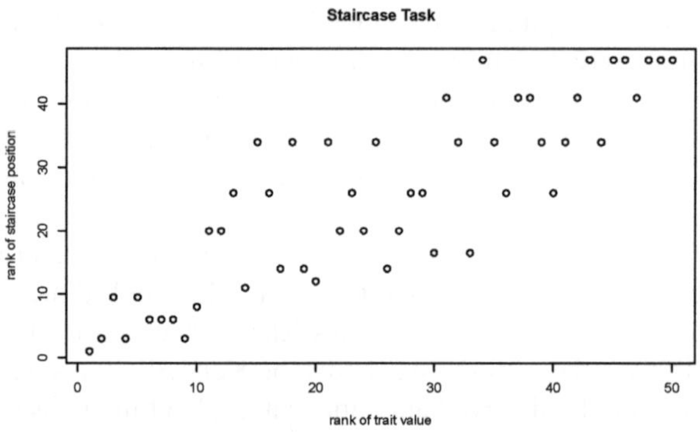

Fig. 4.1 Rank-rank scatter plot showing the relationship between ranked RATF trait scores and ranked behavioral outcomes in the staircase task. Each point represents one persona prompt, with x-axis showing the rank of its trait score and y-axis showing the rank of its final staircase position. The optimized reference point achieves $\tau = 0.70$ out-of-sample correlation, with the positive trend demonstrating systematic behavioral prediction across rank orderings

behavioral information (as evidenced by the significant naive baseline), and mathematical optimization can systematically enhance the extraction of this information (as demonstrated by the optimization improvement). The fact that both approaches achieve statistically significant correlations with behavioral outcomes provides converging evidence for the semantic-behavioral similarity hypothesis central to the Reference-Anchored Trait Framework.

Cross-Task Validation

Cross-task validation provides the critical test of whether reference point optimization discovers genuine behavioral traits or merely task-specific prediction patterns. If the optimized reference point captures fundamental risk preferences rather than staircase-specific behavioral artifacts, it should maintain predictive validity when applied to related decision contexts within the same behavioral domain. This generalization requirement distinguishes true trait discovery from sophisticated overfitting to the training task structure.

We test cross-task generalization using two additional risk preference elicitation procedures implemented with the same persona prompts used in the original staircase experiment. The investment allocation task presents agents with a portfolio choice between a safe asset offering a guaranteed 3% return and a risky asset with a 3% expected return. Each agent makes a single allocation decision, choosing what percentage of their portfolio to invest in the safe versus risky asset. Higher safe asset allocation indicates greater risk aversion, providing a direct measure of risk preferences in a financial decision context.

The insurance staircase task employs the same adaptive binary choice methodology as the original experiment but focuses on insurance purchase decisions rather than lottery versus sure payment choices. Agents face a series of decisions about whether to purchase insurance at varying premium levels. The staircase procedure

Table 4.1 Comparison of trait-based and direct behavioral Kendall's Tau correlations

Task	Trait-based correlation	Direct behavioral correlation (τ) (vs staircase)	Improvement	N
Staircase	0.698	–	–	50
Investment	0.740	0.712	+4%	50
Insurance	0.530	0.362	+46%	50

Note Trait-based Kendall's Tau correlations measure RATF trait scores (from staircase optimization) against each task's behavioral outcomes. Direct behavioral correlations measure behavioral outcomes between task pairs. All correlations significant at $p < 0.001$

adjusts premium amounts based on previous choices, converging on each agent's insurance purchase threshold. Higher willingness to purchase insurance at elevated premiums indicates greater risk aversion, measuring risk preferences through loss domain decisions.

The cross-task validation employs identical persona prompts across all three experimental contexts. The same 50 held-out personas that provided out-of-sample validation for the staircase optimization also participate in both additional tasks. This design ensures that differences in correlation patterns across tasks reflect genuine contextual effects rather than sampling variation across different persona populations.

Table 4.1 presents both the correlations between RATF trait scores and behavioral outcomes, as well as the direct cross-task behavioral correlations. This comparison addresses whether the trait-based correlations merely reflect natural behavioral consistency across risk preference tasks. Recall that the trait scores are computed using the reference point optimized against the staircase task data.

The results demonstrate that the optimized reference point provides predictive validity that exceeds direct cross-task behavioral correlations. The trait measure correlations either match or substantially improve upon direct behavioral correlations, with particularly strong gains for insurance predictions. The trait-based approach achieves $\tau = 0.530$ for insurance prediction compared to only $\tau = 0.362$ for direct staircase-insurance behavioral correlation, representing a 46% improvement. This demonstrates that the optimized reference point captures behavioral information beyond what is accessible through direct cross-task comparison, validating the added value of the trait measurement approach.

The investment allocation task produces the strongest trait-based correlation ($\tau = 0.740$), slightly exceeding both the original discovery task performance ($\tau = 0.698$) and the direct staircase-investment behavioral correlation ($\tau = 0.712$). This finding suggests that the optimized reference point may capture aspects of financial risk preferences that generalize particularly well to portfolio allocation decisions, possibly reflecting the fundamental similarity between lottery evaluation and investment choice mechanisms.

The insurance staircase task yields a meaningful correlation ($\tau = 0.530$) that substantially exceeds the direct cross-task behavioral correlation. This pattern aligns with theoretical expectations, as insurance decisions involve loss domain framing and different psychological mechanisms compared to gain domain lottery choices, even though both contexts tap into underlying risk preference structures. The significant improvement in predictive validity through the trait measure provides evidence that the reference point captures behavioral tendencies that transcend specific decision framings more effectively than direct behavioral comparisons.

These cross-task validation results establish that RATF successfully discovers behaviorally meaningful trait dimensions that provide genuine predictive advantages over task-specific patterns. The consistent predictive validity across experimental contexts, combined with improvements over direct behavioral correlations, demonstrates that the optimized reference point captures generalizable risk preferences in AI agent behavioral patterns while validating the core theoretical assumption that semantic similarity in embedding space corresponds to behavioral similarity across decision contexts. The variation in correlation strength across tasks also reveals how different risk contexts interact with underlying trait dimensions, providing insights for future theoretical development of the framework.

Summary

The Reference-Anchored Trait Framework (RATF) establishes core mathematical principles for discovering behavioral traits through reference point optimization in embedding space. The single-trait approach demonstrates that systematic optimization can meaningfully enhance the extraction of behavioral information from semantic embeddings, achieving a 23% improvement over naive baseline methods. The empirical validation using risk preference data provides concrete evidence that traits discovered through this process capture genuine behavioral patterns rather than task-specific artifacts.

Cross-task validation confirms the framework's practical utility by demonstrating robust generalization across related behavioral contexts. The optimized reference point maintains predictive validity when applied to investment allocation and insurance purchase decisions, with trait-based correlations meeting or exceeding direct behavioral correlations between tasks. This generalization provides strong support for the core hypothesis that semantic similarity in embedding space corresponds to behavioral similarity across decision contexts.

The mathematical foundation established through single-trait RATF enables systematic extension to more complex behavioral analysis scenarios. The framework's emphasis on data-driven trait discovery through optimization provides a template for systematic investigation of behavioral characteristics across diverse domains. This foundation naturally supports simultaneous measurement across multiple behavioral dimensions, setting the stage for comprehensive approaches to persona engineering and behavioral prediction in AI systems.

4.4.3 Mathematical Framework for Multi-trait Persona

The single-trait measurement framework provides a foundation for behavioral trait quantification, but realistic applications require simultaneous measurement across multiple behavioral dimensions. Consider a practical scenario where researchers have discovered a reference point $\mathbf{r}_{\text{risk}}$ for risk preferences through optimization on financial decision tasks. They subsequently want to expand their persona analysis system by adding social trust measurement, requiring a second reference point $\mathbf{r}_{\text{trust}}$ discovered through strategic interaction experiments.

A natural approach might extend personas by concatenating trust-related content to existing risk-focused personas, then apply cosine similarity measurement to each trait independently. However, this approach encounters fundamental geometric limitations. When $\mathbf{r}_{\text{risk}}$ and $\mathbf{r}_{\text{trust}}$ are separated by substantial angular distance in embedding space, no persona embedding can achieve high cosine similarity to both reference points simultaneously. Furthermore, if persona1 exhibits higher risk aversion than persona2, adding trust-related content to both personas requires renormalization to unit length, which could potentially alter the risk ranking between the two personas despite the addition of semantically orthogonal content.

The mathematical framework developed here addresses these challenges through a subspace projection approach that enables stable, interpretable measurement across multiple trait dimensions while preserving ranking relationships during trait expansion. The method assumes that personas contain only content related to the measured behavioral traits, providing theoretical guarantees within this constrained but practically relevant setting.

Mathematical Setup and Notation

Consider N behavioral traits, each represented by a unit-norm reference point $\mathbf{r}_1, \mathbf{r}_2, \ldots, \mathbf{r}_N \in \mathbb{R}^d$ discovered through single-trait optimization procedures. Let $R = [\mathbf{r}_1, \mathbf{r}_2, \ldots, \mathbf{r}_N] \in \mathbb{R}^{d\times N}$ denote the matrix of reference points, and define the trait subspace $S = \text{span}\{\mathbf{r}_1, \mathbf{r}_2, \ldots, \mathbf{r}_N\} \subseteq \mathbb{R}^d$. Assume the reference points are linearly independent, so $\text{rank}(R) = N$ and $\dim(S) = N$.

The challenge arises when reference points are not orthogonal. Direct application of cosine similarity $\mathbf{x}^\top \mathbf{r}_i$ to each trait creates dependencies between measurements and fails to provide a systematic framework for handling the geometric constraints of unit-norm embeddings across multiple dimensions.

Definition 4.1 (*Löwdin orthonormalization of reference points*). Let the compact singular value decomposition be $R = U\Sigma V^\top$ with $U \in \mathbb{R}^{d\times N}, \Sigma = \text{diag}(\sigma_1, \ldots, \sigma_N) > 0$, and $V \in \mathbb{R}^{N\times N}$. Define

$$Q := UV^\top = R(R^\top R)^{-1/2} \in \mathbb{R}^{d\times N} \tag{4.7}$$

The columns $\mathbf{q}_1, \ldots, \mathbf{q}_N$ of Q form an orthonormal basis of S.

Lemma 4.1 (Properties of orthonormal basis). $Q^\top Q = I_N$, $col(Q) = S$.

Proof From the SVD $R = U\Sigma V^\top$, we have $R^\top R = V\Sigma^2 V^\top$ and $(R^\top R)^{-1/2} = V\Sigma^{-1}V^\top$. Therefore $Q = R(R^\top R)^{-1/2} = U\Sigma V^\top V\Sigma^{-1}V^\top = UV^\top$, which gives $Q^\top Q = VU^\top UV^\top = I_N$ and $\mathrm{col}(Q) = \mathrm{col}(U) = S$.

This construction transforms potentially correlated reference points into an orthogonal coordinate system while preserving the geometric structure of the trait subspace.

Multi-Trait Measurement via Trait Scores

Definition 4.2 (*Trait scores*) Given the orthonormal basis $Q = [\mathbf{q}_1, \ldots, \mathbf{q}_N]$, the trait measurements are:

$$\mathrm{trait}_i(\mathbf{x}) = \mathbf{x}^\top \mathbf{q}_i \quad \text{for } i = 1, \ldots, N \tag{4.8}$$

These trait scores measure trait intensity along each pseudo-trait dimension.

Connection to Single-Trait Cosine Similarity. When $N = 1$, we have a single reference point $\mathbf{r}_1$. The orthonormalization produces $Q = [\mathbf{r}_1]$ (since $\mathbf{r}_1$ is already unit-norm), and the trait measurement reduces to $\mathrm{trait}_1(\mathbf{x}) = \mathbf{x}^\top \mathbf{q}_1 = \mathbf{x}^\top \mathbf{r}_1$, which is exactly the original cosine similarity measure. The multi-trait framework thus represents a principled extension rather than a replacement of the single-trait approach.

Ranking Preservation Under Trait Expansion

A central application involves expanding personas from fewer traits to more traits while preserving established rankings.

Theorem 4.1 (Ranking preservation under trait expansion). Consider personas initially constructed within subspace $S_1 = \mathrm{span}\{\mathbf{r}_1, \ldots, \mathbf{r}_m\}$ and subsequently expanded to $S_2 = \mathrm{span}\{\mathbf{r}_1, \ldots, \mathbf{r}_m, \mathbf{r}_{m+1}, \ldots, \mathbf{r}_N\}$. Assume:

(i) *Block orthogonality of reference points*: $\mathbf{r}_i^\top \mathbf{r}_j = 0$ for all $i \le m$ and $j > m$.
(ii) *Orthogonal unit-norm persona expansion*: for each persona $\mathbf{x}$ the expanded persona is

$$\mathbf{x}' = \frac{\mathbf{x} + \mathbf{w}_x}{\|\mathbf{x} + \mathbf{w}_x\|},$$

where $\mathbf{w}_x$ is a unit vector in $S_1^\perp$. The expansion vector is allowed to depend on the persona.

Let Q_1, Q_2 denote the Löwdin orthonormal bases of S_1 and S_2 respectively, and $\mathrm{trait}_i^{(1)}$, $\mathrm{trait}_i^{(2)}$ the corresponding trait scores. Then for every pair of unit-norm personas $\mathbf{x}, \mathbf{y} \in S_1$, with expanded personas $\mathbf{x}' = (\mathbf{x} + \mathbf{w}_x)/\|\mathbf{x} + \mathbf{w}_x\|$ and $\mathbf{y}' = (\mathbf{y} + \mathbf{w}_y)/\|\mathbf{y} + \mathbf{w}_y\|$,

$$\mathrm{trait}_i^{(1)}(\mathbf{x}) > \mathrm{trait}_i^{(1)}(\mathbf{y}) \iff \mathrm{trait}_i^{(2)}(\mathbf{x}') > \mathrm{trait}_i^{(2)}(\mathbf{y}') \tag{4.9}$$

for $i = 1, \ldots, m$.

Proof Under assumption (i), the Gram matrix $G_2 = R_2^\top R_2$ is block diagonal: $G_2 = \mathrm{diag}(G_1, G')$, where $G_1 = R_1^\top R_1$ and G' is the Gram matrix of $\mathbf{r}_{m+1}, ..., \mathbf{r}_N$. Hence $G_2^{-1/2} = \mathrm{diag}(G_1^{-1/2}, G'^{-1/2})$, and

$$Q_2 = R_2 G_2^{-1/2} = [R_1|R']\mathrm{diag}(G_1^{-1/2}, G'^{-1/2}) = [R_1 G_1^{-1/2}|R'G'^{-1/2}] = [Q_1|Q'].$$

In particular, $\mathbf{q}_i^{(2)} = \mathbf{q}_i^{(1)} \in S_1$ for $i = 1, ..., m$.

Let $\mathbf{x}, \mathbf{y} \in S_1$ be unit-norm personas and let $\mathbf{w}_x, \mathbf{w}_y$ be their expansion vectors, each a unit vector in $S_1^\perp$ by assumption (ii). The expanded personas are $\mathbf{x}' = (\mathbf{x} + \mathbf{w}_x)/\|\mathbf{x} + \mathbf{w}_x\|$ and $\mathbf{y}' = (\mathbf{y} + \mathbf{w}_y)/\|\mathbf{y} + \mathbf{w}_y\|$. Since $\mathbf{w}_x \in S_1^\perp$ and $\mathbf{x} \in S_1$, $\mathbf{x}^\top \mathbf{w}_x = 0$ and

$$\|\mathbf{x} + \mathbf{w}_x\|^2 = \|\mathbf{x}\|^2 + \|\mathbf{w}_x\|^2 = 1 + 1 = 2.$$

The same computation gives $\|\mathbf{y} + \mathbf{w}_y\|^2 = 2$. The renormalization factor is therefore $1/\sqrt{2}$ for both personas, independent of the direction of $\mathbf{w}_x$ and $\mathbf{w}_y$ within $S_1^\perp$.

For $i = 1, ..., m$, using $\mathbf{q}_i^{(2)} = \mathbf{q}_i^{(1)} \in S_1$ and $\mathbf{w}_x^\top \mathbf{q}_i^{(1)} = 0$,

$$\mathrm{trait}_i^{(2)}(\mathbf{x}') = \frac{(\mathbf{x} + \mathbf{w}_x)^\top \mathbf{q}_i^{(1)}}{\|\mathbf{x} + \mathbf{w}_x\|} = \frac{\mathbf{x}^\top \mathbf{q}_i^{(1)}}{\sqrt{2}} = \frac{1}{\sqrt{2}}\mathrm{trait}_i^{(1)}(\mathbf{x}).$$

The analogous identity, $\mathrm{trait}_i^{(2)}(\mathbf{y}') = \frac{1}{\sqrt{2}}\mathrm{trait}_i^{(1)}(\mathbf{y})$, follows identically with $\mathbf{y}$ and $\mathbf{w}_y$ in place of $\mathbf{x}$ and $\mathbf{w}_x$. Multiplying both sides of a strict inequality by a common positive constant preserves the inequality, so the ranking on the first m trait imensions is preserved. □

This theorem guarantees that adding new trait dimensions (such as expanding from risk-only to risk-plus-trust personas) preserves the behavioral rankings established in the original analysis.

Orthogonal and Non-Orthogonal Persona Expansion

Theorem 4.1 governs *orthogonal persona expansion*, in which the added content vector $\mathbf{w}_x$ for each persona lies in $S_1^\perp$ and introduces no projection onto the original trait sub-space. A different regime, *non-orthogonal persona expansion*, arises when the embedding of the added text has a non-zero component inside S_1. Decomposing $\mathbf{w}_x = \mathbf{w}_{x,\|}\mathbf{w}_{x,\perp}$ with $\mathbf{w}_{x,\|} \in S_1$ and $\mathbf{w}_{x,\perp} \in S_1^\perp$, the expanded trait scores on the first m dimensions pick up a shift proportional to $\mathbf{w}_{x,\|}^\top \mathbf{q}_i^{(1)}$, modulated by the renormalization factor. This shift is not a measurement artifact; it registers that the added text carries content aligned with the existing traits, even when the text was intended to introduce a newly defined trait.

For instance, consider a persona describing an altruistic agent, to which the text 'you are a fair person' is appended. Although the added text nominally targets a fairness trait, its embedding has a non-trivial projection onto the altruism reference direction because fairness and altruism share semantic content in embedding space. The resulting shift in altruism scores reflects this semantic overlap rather than an instability of the measurement procedure.

The framework thus distinguishes two cases. Orthogonal persona expansion is the regime in which Theorem 4.1 applies and rankings on the original traits are preserved under a common positive rescaling. Non-orthogonal persona expansion is the regime in which trait scores on the original dimensions shift, with those shifts carrying behavioral meaning about the semantic content of the added text.

Recovery of Original Reference Point Measurements

When reference points are not orthogonal, the trait scores represent measurements in the orthonormalized coordinate system rather than direct projections onto original reference points. The following result enables exact recovery of original reference point relationships.

Proposition 4.1 (Conversion between orthogonal and original coordinates) *Let $G := R^\top R \in \mathbb{R}^{N\times N}$ be the Gram matrix of reference points. The relationships between trait scores $\boldsymbol{\tau}(\mathbf{x}) = [trait_1(\mathbf{x}), \ldots, trait_N(\mathbf{x})]^\top$ and original reference projections $\mathbf{s}(\mathbf{x}) = R^\top \mathbf{x}$ are:*

$$\boldsymbol{\tau}(\mathbf{x}) = G^{-1/2}\mathbf{s}(\mathbf{x}) \quad \text{and} \quad \mathbf{s}(\mathbf{x}) = G^{1/2}\boldsymbol{\tau}(\mathbf{x}) \tag{4.10}$$

Proof From the orthonormalization $Q = RG^{-1/2}$, we have $\boldsymbol{\tau}(\mathbf{x}) = Q^\top \mathbf{x} = G^{-1/2} R^\top \mathbf{x} = G^{-1/2}\mathbf{s}(\mathbf{x})$. The reverse relationship follows by applying $G^{1/2}$ to both sides. □

This conversion enables interpretation of trait measurements in terms of the original reference points while maintaining the mathematical advantages of orthogonal coordinates for stable multi-trait measurement.

Assumptions and Limitations

The framework assumes that personas are constructed to contain only behavioral trait information, with all semantic content lying within the trait subspace S. The approach further assumes completeness of the trait space, requiring that the reference points capture all relevant behavioral dimensions for the intended application domain.

The mathematical framework presented here is purely theoretical and lacks empirical validation. The robustness properties when assumptions are violated remain unknown. For instance, real-world embedding processes introduce noise and small amounts of content orthogonal to the trait subspace, but the framework's tolerance to such violations has not been characterized. Similarly, the practical impact of incomplete trait spaces or imperfect persona construction on measurement quality requires empirical investigation. Future work must address these robustness questions and validate the theoretical predictions through systematic experimentation with constructed personas and behavioral validation tasks.

Theorem 4.1 relies in addition on the *additive embedding model*, in which the embedding of a concatenated text string equals the sum of the embeddings of its components. This assumption underwrites the decomposition $\mathbf{x}' \propto \mathbf{x} + \mathbf{w}_x$ used in the expansion operator. The additive model is motivated by the compositional semantics literature, where additive composition of distributional vectors provides a strong baseline for sentence meaning (Mitchell and Lapata, 2010; Arora, Liang, and Ma, 2017), and by the linear representation hypothesis for large language models (Park, Choe, and Veitch, 2024). It is nevertheless an idealization: modern transformer embeddings of concatenated text are nonlinear functions of the full input, so the identity $\text{embed}(s_1 \| s_2) = \text{embed}(s_1) + \text{embed}(s_2)$ holds only approximately. Empirical characterization of the approximation error, and its effect on the $1/\sqrt{2}$ rescaling factor in Theorem 4.1, is left to future work.

4.5 Conclusion

This chapter presents the Embedding-Based Trait Theory (EBTT), a proposed mathematical framework for connecting persona prompts to behavioral predictions in AI systems. The theory advances a four-stage pipeline that transforms linguistic inputs through embeddings and traits to behavioral outputs, providing the first systematic mathematical approach to persona engineering in artificial intelligence. While we present a systematic theoretical framework, the empirical validation remains limited, representing initial proof-of-concept rather than established scientific consensus.

The Reference-Anchored Trait Framework (RATF) constitutes the core theoretical contribution, proposing that behavioral traits can be measured through similarity to empirically discovered reference points in embedding space. The single-trait implementation demonstrates mathematical feasibility through risk preference analysis, achieving meaningful improvements over baseline methods and showing cross-task generalization across three related decision contexts. However, this validation represents a narrow empirical foundation involving a single behavioral domain, limited sample sizes, and tasks within the same conceptual category. The framework's broader applicability across diverse behavioral dimensions, AI architectures, and decision contexts remains an open empirical question requiring systematic investigation.

The multi-trait mathematical framework extends the single-trait foundation to enable simultaneous measurement across multiple behavioral dimensions. The Löwdin orthonormalization approach provides principled handling of correlated reference points, while the ranking preservation theorem offers theoretical guarantees for systematic trait expansion in practical applications. This mathematical machinery addresses fundamental challenges in scaling from simple to complex persona engineering scenarios. Nevertheless, the multi-trait framework remains entirely theoretical, lacking any empirical validation. The mathematical elegance and theoretical completeness cannot substitute for the systematic empirical investigation needed to establish the framework's practical utility and behavioral validity.

The theoretical development significantly outpaces empirical validation throughout this work. While the mathematical foundations provide a rigorous starting point and the initial proof-of-concept provides encouraging evidence for core assumptions, extensive validation is required before the framework can support reliable practical applications. The semantic-behavioral similarity hypothesis underlying RATF requires testing across diverse domains, the cross-architecture portability of trait measurements needs systematic investigation, and the robustness properties of multi-trait measurement remain unexplored. Additionally, the framework's assumptions about persona construction, trait subspace completeness, and embedding stability require empirical verification under realistic deployment conditions.

The primary contribution of this chapter lies in establishing a research agenda rather than providing definitive solutions. The mathematical framework creates a foundation for systematic empirical investigation of AI behavioral patterns while the initial validation demonstrates research feasibility and methodological potential. Future work must address the substantial gap between theoretical development and empirical evidence through comprehensive validation studies, cross-domain replication, and systematic comparison across AI architectures. The framework's ultimate value will depend on its ability to enable reliable behavioral prediction and control in practical AI deployment scenarios.

EBTT represents a step toward transforming persona engineering from an art to a science through mathematical rigor and empirical validation. The theoretical foundations developed here provide the conceptual tools necessary for systematic investigation of AI behavioral patterns, while the limited empirical results suggest promising directions for future research. However, significant theoretical and empirical work remains before these ideas can support robust practical applications or contribute to broader scientific understanding of artificial intelligence behavior.

Appendix A: Spherical Coordinate Descent Optimization Algorithm

4.6 Problem Formulation and Objective Function

The optimization problem underlying the Reference-Anchored Trait Framework seeks to discover reference points $\mathbf{r} \in \mathbb{S}^{1535}$ that maximize the correlation between semantic similarity (measured via cosine similarity) and behavioral similarity (measured via staircase task outcomes). This section details the mathematical formulation of the optimization objective and the rationale behind our design choices.

4.6.1 Soft Kendall's Tau Objective Function

Rather than optimizing the classical Kendall's tau directly, we employ a smoothed version that enables continuous optimization while preserving the essential rank-correlation properties. The soft Kendall's tau objective function is defined as:

$$\text{objective}(\mathbf{r}) = 1 - \tau_{\text{soft}}(\mathbf{r}) \tag{4.11}$$

where τ_{soft} is computed as follows. For a reference point $\mathbf{r}$ and embedding matrix $\mathbf{X} \in \mathbb{R}^{n \times 1536}$, we first compute cosine similarities:

$$s_i = \frac{\mathbf{x}_i^\top \mathbf{r}}{||\mathbf{x}_i||_2 \cdot ||\mathbf{r}||_2} = \mathbf{x}_i^\top \mathbf{r} \tag{4.12}$$

since both embeddings and reference points are unit-normalized. Let $y_1, \ldots, y_n$ denote the corresponding behavioral outcomes (staircase positions). We then compute pairwise differences:

$$\Delta s_{ij} = s_i - s_j \tag{4.13}$$

$$\Delta y_{ij} = y_i - y_j \tag{4.14}$$

The soft Kendall's tau employs tanh smoothing to approximate the sign function:

$$\tilde{s}_{ij} = \tanh\left(\frac{\Delta s_{ij}}{\sigma_s}\right) \tag{4.15}$$

$$\tilde{y}_{ij} = \tanh\left(\frac{\Delta y_{ij}}{\sigma_y}\right) \tag{4.16}$$

where σ_s and σ_y are smoothing parameters. The soft Kendall's tau coefficient is then:

$$\tau_{\text{soft}} = \frac{\sum_{i<j} \tilde{s}_{ij} \tilde{y}_{ij}}{\sqrt{\sum_{i<j} |\tilde{s}_{ij}| \cdot \sum_{i<j} |\tilde{y}_{ij}|}} \tag{4.17}$$

4.6.2 Adaptive Smoothing Parameter Selection

When smoothing parameters are not provided, they are set adaptively from the data:

$$\sigma_s = \text{median}\{|\Delta s_{ij}| : i < j, |\Delta s_{ij}| > 0\} \tag{4.18}$$

$$\sigma_y = \text{median}\{|\Delta y_{ij}| : i < j, |\Delta y_{ij}| > 0\} \tag{4.19}$$

This adaptive approach ensures that the smoothing is appropriately scaled to the data while maintaining numerical stability. In our implementation, we used $\sigma = 0.05$ based on empirical performance across different optimization runs.

4.6.3 *Objective Function Properties*

The soft Kendall's tau objective has several important properties:

- **Range**: $\tau_{\text{soft}} \in [-1, 1]$, so the objective function ranges in [0, 2]
- **Smoothness**: Unlike classical Kendall's tau, the soft version is differentiable almost everywhere
- **Multi-modality**: The rank-based nature still creates multiple local optima
- **Interpretation**: Values closer to 0 indicate stronger positive correlation

4.7 Why Spherical Coordinate Descent Was Chosen

The choice of spherical coordinate descent over gradient-based optimization methods reflects several fundamental challenges that make standard approaches computationally intractable or theoretically problematic for this optimization landscape.

4.7.1 *Dimensionality Challenge*

The embedding space dimensionality of $d = 1536$ creates a high-dimensional optimization problem on the unit sphere $\mathbb{S}^{1535}$. Gradient-based methods for manifold optimization face several scaling challenges:

- **Computational complexity**: Computing the Riemannian gradient requires $O(d^2)$ operations for each gradient step
- **Memory requirements**: Storing approximations to the Riemannian Hessian requires $O(d^2)$ memory
- **Numerical instability**: High-dimensional manifold operations suffer from accumulated floating-point errors

In contrast, coordinate descent reduces each step to a one-dimensional optimization problem, requiring only $O(d)$ operations per coordinate update.

4.7.2 *Gradient Complexity of Soft Kendall's Tau*

Computing gradients of the soft Kendall's tau objective involves several layers of complexity:

1. **Pairwise operations**: The objective depends on $O(n^2)$ pairwise differences
2. **Chain rule through tanh**: Each pairwise term requires differentiation of $\tanh(\Delta s_{ij}/\sigma)$ where Δs_{ij} itself depends on the reference point

3. **Normalization terms**: The denominator in the soft Kendall's tau formula requires additional chain rule applications
4. **Manifold constraints**: Maintaining the unit sphere constraint requires projecting gradients to the tangent space

The resulting gradient expression is computationally expensive and prone to numerical errors, particularly in high dimensions.

4.7.3 Multi-modal Objective Landscape

The rank-based nature of Kendall's tau, even in its smoothed form, creates an objective landscape with multiple local optima. This multi-modality arises because:

- Small changes in the reference point can cause discrete changes in rank orderings
- Different regions of embedding space may contain equivalent behavioral information
- The softening parameter σ creates smooth transitions but does not eliminate local optima

Gradient-based methods typically get trapped in local optima, while the grid search component of coordinate descent provides better global exploration.

4.7.4 Implementation Pragmatism

Spherical coordinate descent avoids the substantial implementation complexity of Riemannian optimization:

- **No differential geometry**: Avoids implementing exponential maps, retractions, or parallel transport
- **Automatic constraint satisfaction**: Great circle parameterization maintains unit length automatically
- **Modular design**: One-dimensional optimization routines can be optimized and tested independently
- **Debugging simplicity**: Each coordinate update can be inspected and validated separately

4.8 Great Circle Parameterization

The mathematical foundation of our approach relies on parameterizing movement on the unit sphere through great circles, which provides a natural way to perform one-dimensional optimization while maintaining the spherical constraint.

4.8.1 Mathematical Formulation

For optimization along coordinate i, given current reference point $\mathbf{r} \in \mathbb{S}^{1535}$, we construct the parameterization:

$$\mathbf{r}(\theta) = \mathbf{r}\cos(\theta) + \mathbf{v}\sin(\theta) \tag{4.20}$$

where $\mathbf{v}$ is the normalized orthogonal direction:

$$\mathbf{e}_i = i\text{-th coordinate unit vector} \tag{4.21}$$

$$\mathbf{u} = \mathbf{e}_i - (\mathbf{e}_i^\top \mathbf{r})\mathbf{r} \tag{4.22}$$

$$\mathbf{v} = \frac{\mathbf{u}}{||\mathbf{u}||_2} \tag{4.23}$$

This construction ensures that:

- $||\mathbf{r}(\theta)||_2 = 1$ for all θ (automatic unit constraint)
- $\mathbf{r}(0) = \mathbf{r}$ (starting point preservation)
- The path traces a great circle in the 2-dimensional subspace spanned by $\mathbf{r}$ and $\mathbf{e}_i$

4.8.2 Geometric Interpretation

The great circle parameterization has several geometric advantages:

- **Geodesic paths**: Great circles are the shortest paths on the sphere surface
- **Natural parameterization**: The angle θ provides intuitive distance measurement
- **Full coverage**: For $\theta \in [0, 2\pi)$, the parameterization covers all points on the great circle
- **Numerical stability**: Trigonometric functions are numerically stable and well-conditioned

4.8.3 Degenerate Cases

When $||\mathbf{u}||_2 < 10^{-12}$ (indicating $\mathbf{r}$ is already aligned with $\mathbf{e}_i$), no meaningful rotation exists within the subspace. In such cases, the algorithm returns the current reference point without modification, ensuring numerical stability.

4.9 Two-Phase Optimization Strategy for One-Dimensional Subproblems

Each coordinate update requires solving a one-dimensional optimization problem along a great circle arc. Due to the multi-modal nature of the soft Kendall's tau objective, we employ a sophisticated two-phase strategy that combines global exploration with precise local refinement.

4.9.1 Overview of the Two-Phase Approach

The one-dimensional optimization proceeds through two sequential phases:

1. **Phase 1 - Global Grid Search**: Systematic exploration over the entire parameter space $\theta \in [0, 2\pi)$ to identify promising regions
2. **Phase 2 - Local Refinement**: Precise optimization within promising regions using R's built-in `optimize()` function

This hybrid approach leverages the complementary strengths of both methods: grid search provides robust global exploration that avoids missing important optima, while sophisticated local optimization achieves high precision in the final solution.

4.9.2 Phase 1: Coarse Grid Search

The first phase performs systematic exploration over the entire parameter space:

Grid Construction

The interval $[0, 2\pi)$ is divided into $G = 64$ equally-spaced evaluation points:

$$\theta_g = \frac{2\pi g}{G}, \quad g = 0, 1, 2, \ldots, G - 1 \tag{4.24}$$

Note that we exclude $\theta = 2\pi$ to avoid duplication with $\theta = 0$ on the periodic domain.

Objective Evaluation

For each grid point θ_g, we evaluate the objective function:

$$f_g = \text{SoftKendall}(\mathbf{r}\cos(\theta_g) + \mathbf{v}\sin(\theta_g)) \tag{4.25}$$

This requires $G = 64$ complete evaluations of the soft Kendall's tau function, each involving $O(n^2)$ pairwise operations.

Candidate Selection

From the G evaluations, we select the $K = 2$ grid points with the lowest objective values:

$$\{\theta_{g_1}, \theta_{g_2}\} = \arg \min_{K \text{ distinct}} \{f_0, f_1, \ldots, f_{G-1}\} \tag{4.26}$$

These represent the most promising regions for further refinement.

4.9.3 Phase 2: Local Refinement Using R's `optimize()` Function

The second phase performs precise optimization around each promising candidate identified in Phase 1.

R's `optimize()` Function

R's built-in `optimize()` function implements a hybrid algorithm combining:

- **Golden-section search**: Robust method that requires no derivative information
- **Parabolic interpolation**: Accelerates convergence when the function is smooth
- **Automatic bracketing**: Handles boundary conditions and maintains search intervals

The function signature is:

```
optimize(f, interval, tol = .Machine$double.eps^0.25, maximum = FALSE)
```

where `f` is the objective function, `interval` is the search bracket, and `tol` controls convergence precision.

Bracket Construction

For each promising grid point θ_{g_i}, we construct a local search bracket:

$$\text{bracket}_i = [\theta_{g_i} - \delta, \theta_{g_i} + \delta] \tag{4.27}$$

where $\delta = \frac{2\pi}{G}$ is the grid spacing. This creates overlapping intervals around each candidate, ensuring that optima near grid boundaries are not missed.

Boundary Handling

Since θ is periodic on $[0, 2\pi)$, brackets that extend beyond the domain boundaries require special handling:

- **Lower boundary**: If $\theta_{g_i} - \delta < 0$, the bracket becomes $[\theta_{g_i} - \delta + 2\pi, 2\pi) \cup [0, \theta_{g_i} + \delta]$
- **Upper boundary**: If $\theta_{g_i} + \delta \geq 2\pi$, the bracket becomes $[\theta_{g_i} - \delta, 2\pi) \cup [0, \theta_{g_i} + \delta - 2\pi]$

In practice, we handle this by defining the objective function to accept any real-valued θ and automatically wrap it to $[0, 2\pi)$ internally.

Local Optimization Process

For each bracket, we invoke R's `optimize()` function:

```
result <- optimize(theta_objective, interval = bracket_i, tol = 1e-8)
```

where `theta_objective` is a wrapper function that:

1. Wraps the input angle θ to $[0, 2\pi)$
2. Computes $\mathbf{r}(\theta) = \mathbf{r}\cos(\theta) + \mathbf{v}\sin(\theta)$
3. Evaluates the soft Kendall's tau objective function
4. Returns the objective value

4.9.4 Final Selection

After completing local optimization around all K promising candidates, we select the overall best result:

$$\theta^* = \arg\min_{i=1,\ldots,K} \text{optimize\_result}_i.\text{objective} \tag{4.28}$$

The final optimized reference point is then:

$$\mathbf{r}^* = \mathbf{r}\cos(\theta^*) + \mathbf{v}\sin(\theta^*) \tag{4.29}$$

4.9.5 Computational Complexity of Two-Phase Strategy

The computational cost of each one-dimensional optimization is:

- **Phase 1**: $O(G \cdot n^2) = O(64 \cdot n^2)$ for grid search
- **Phase 2**: $O(K \cdot L \cdot n^2) = O(2 \cdot L \cdot n^2)$ where L is the number of iterations for each local optimization

Since L is typically 10-20 iterations for the specified tolerance, the total cost is $O((G + KL) \cdot n^2) \approx O(100 \cdot n^2)$ per coordinate update.

4.9.6 Why This Two-Phase Approach Works

The hybrid strategy is effective because:

1. **Global coverage**: Grid search ensures no major optima are missed due to poor initialization
2. **Multi-modal handling**: Multiple local refinements explore different basins of attraction
3. **Precision**: R's `optimize()` achieves high precision (typically 8-10 significant digits)
4. **Robustness**: Golden-section search works reliably even with noisy or irregular objective functions
5. **Efficiency**: Local refinement only in promising regions avoids wasted computation

4.10 Efficiency Enhancements

Several algorithmic enhancements address the computational challenges of high-dimensional optimization while maintaining solution quality.

4.10.1 Active Set Management

Rather than cycling through all 1536 dimensions at each iteration, the algorithm maintains an active set of promising dimensions:

- **Active set size**: $A = 512$ dimensions (approximately one-third of total)
- **Initialization**: Begin with random subset of dimensions
- **Refresh frequency**: Update active set every $R = 256$ iterations
- **Performance tracking**: Maintain improvement statistics for each dimension

4.10.2 UCB Bandit Selection Strategy

Dimension selection within the active set follows an Upper Confidence Bound (UCB) strategy:

$$\text{UCB}_i = \bar{\mu}_i + c\sqrt{\frac{\ln t}{n_i}} \tag{4.30}$$

where:

- $\bar{\mu}_i$: Average improvement achieved by dimension i
- $c = 1.0$: Exploration constant
- t: Total number of iterations
- n_i: Number of times dimension i has been selected

This approach balances exploitation of high-performing dimensions with exploration of under-sampled coordinates.

4.10.3 Statistical Decay

To adapt to non-stationary optimization landscapes, improvement statistics are updated with exponential decay:

$$\bar{\mu}_i \leftarrow \rho\bar{\mu}_i + (1 - \rho)\text{improvement}_i \tag{4.31}$$

with decay factor $\rho = 0.97$, ensuring that recent performance has higher influence than historical averages.

4.10.4 Computational Complexity Analysis

The complexity per iteration is:

- **Active set management**: $O(A)$ for dimension selection
- **Great circle construction**: $O(d)$ for orthogonal vector computation
- **Two-phase optimization**: $O((G + KL) \cdot n^2) \approx O(100 \cdot n^2)$ for complete 1D optimization

The total per-iteration complexity is $O(100 \cdot n^2 + d + A) \approx O(n^2)$, which is manageable for our problem size of $n = 50$ training observations and $d = 1536$ dimensions.

4.11 Convergence and Stopping Criteria

The algorithm incorporates multiple convergence detection and early stopping mechanisms to ensure efficient termination while maintaining solution quality.

4.11.1 Improvement-Based Stopping

The primary stopping criterion monitors objective function improvement:

- **Minimum absolute improvement**: $\Delta_{\text{abs}} = 10^{-8}$
- **Minimum relative improvement**: $\Delta_{\text{rel}} = 10^{-4} \cdot |f(\mathbf{r}_0)|$
- **Evaluation frequency**: Check every iteration

Optimization terminates when improvement falls below both thresholds for consecutive iterations.

4.11.2 Validation-Based Early Stopping

Optional validation-based stopping uses held-out data:

- **Validation frequency**: Every 100 iterations
- **Patience parameter**: $p = 5$ validation checks without improvement
- **Best model retention**: Store reference point achieving best validation performance

This mechanism prevents overfitting to the training data while maintaining generalization performance.

4.11.3 Maximum Iteration Limits

Hard limits prevent excessive computation:

- **Maximum iterations**: $I_{\max} = 500$
- **Time limits**: Optional wall-clock time constraints
- **Resource monitoring**: Memory usage tracking for large-scale applications

4.11.4 Convergence Diagnostics

The algorithm provides several diagnostic measures:

- **Improvement trajectory**: Objective function values over iterations

- **Dimension activity**: Frequency of selection for each coordinate
- **UCB statistics**: Exploration vs. exploitation balance
- **Validation performance**: Out-of-sample correlation tracking

4.12 Implementation Details

This section covers the specific hyperparameter settings, numerical considerations, and implementation choices that ensure robust performance across different problem instances.

4.12.1 Hyperparameter Settings

The following hyperparameters were used in our implementation:

Parameter	**Value**	**Description**
σ	0.05	Soft Kendall's tau smoothing parameter
G	64	Grid search resolution
K	2	Number of candidates for local refinement
A	512	Active set size
R	256	Active set refresh frequency
c	1.0	UCB exploration constant
ρ	0.97	Statistical decay factor
ϵ	10^{-8}	Local optimization tolerance
Δ_{abs}	10^{-8}	Minimum absolute improvement
Δ_{rel}	10^{-4}	Minimum relative improvement
$I_{\max}$	500	Maximum iterations
p	5	Validation patience

4.12.2 Numerical Stability Considerations

Several measures ensure numerical robustness:

- **Unit norm maintenance**: Explicit renormalization after each great circle step
- **Degeneracy detection**: Check for near-zero orthogonal vectors ($||\mathbf{u}||_2 < 10^{-12}$)
- **Objective bounds**: Clamp objective values to valid ranges [0, 2]
- **Angle wrapping**: Ensure $\theta \in [0, 2\pi)$ for great circle parameterization

4.12.3 Memory Management

Efficient memory usage is achieved through:

- **Sparse storage**: Store only upper triangular pairwise differences
- **Streaming computation**: Process pairwise terms without full matrix storage
- **History truncation**: Limit stored optimization history to recent iterations

4.12.4 Error Handling

Robust error handling covers common failure modes:

- **Optimization failures**: Fallback to best grid point when local optimization fails
- **Numerical overflow**: Clamp intermediate computations to valid ranges
- **Invalid inputs**: Validate embedding matrices and behavioral outcome vectors

4.13 Algorithm Pseudocode

Algorithm 14.1 Spherical Coordinate Descent for Reference Point Optimization

Require: Embedding matrix $\mathbf{X} \in \mathbb{R}^{n \times d}$, behavioral outcomes $\mathbf{y} \in \mathbb{R}^n$, initial reference point $\mathbf{r}_0$
Ensure: Optimized reference point $\mathbf{r}^*$

$\mathbf{r} \leftarrow \mathbf{r}_0/||\mathbf{r}_0||_2$ {Normalize initial point}
$f_{\text{best}} \leftarrow$ SoftKendall($\mathbf{r}, \mathbf{X}, \mathbf{y}$)
$\mathcal{A} \leftarrow$ RandomSubset($1, \ldots, d, A$) {Initialize active set}
Initialize UCB statistics: $\bar{\mu}_i \leftarrow 0, n_i \leftarrow 0$ for all i
for $t = 1$ to $I_{\max}$ **do**
  if $t \bmod R = 0$ **then**
    $\mathcal{A} \leftarrow$ RefreshActiveSet($\mathcal{A}, \bar{\mu}, n$)
  end if
  $i^* \leftarrow \arg\max_{i \in \mathcal{A}} \text{UCB}(\bar{\mu}_i, n_i, t, c)$
  $\mathbf{r}_{\text{new}}, f_{\text{new}} \leftarrow$ TwoPhaseDimensionOptimization($\mathbf{r}, i^*, \mathbf{X}, \mathbf{y}$)
  improvement $\leftarrow f_{\text{best}} - f_{\text{new}}$
  if improvement > 0 **then**
    $\mathbf{r} \leftarrow \mathbf{r}_{\text{new}}$
    $f_{\text{best}} \leftarrow f_{\text{new}}$
  end if
  Update UCB statistics: $\bar{\mu}_{i^*} \leftarrow \rho\bar{\mu}_{i^*} + (1-\rho) \cdot$ improvement
  $n_{i^*} \leftarrow n_{i^*} + 1$
  if improvement $< \Delta_{\text{abs}}$ AND improvement $< \Delta_{\text{rel}} \cdot |f(\mathbf{r}_0)|$ **then**
    break {Convergence achieved}
  end if
  if $t \bmod 100 = 0$ AND validation enabled **then**
    Evaluate validation performance and check for early stopping
  end if
end for
return r

Algorithm 14.2 Two-Phase One-Dimensional Optimization Along Great Circle

Require: Current reference point $\mathbf{r}$, coordinate index i, data $\mathbf{X}$, $\mathbf{y}$
Ensure: Optimized reference point $\mathbf{r}^*$, objective value f^*

$\mathbf{e}_i \leftarrow$ coordinate unit vector for dimension i
$\mathbf{u} \leftarrow \mathbf{e}_i - (\mathbf{e}_i^\top \mathbf{r})\mathbf{r}$
if $||\mathbf{u}||_2 < 10^{-12}$ **then**
  {Degenerate case}
  return $\mathbf{r}$, SOFTKENDALL($\mathbf{r}$, $\mathbf{X}$, $\mathbf{y}$)
end if
$\mathbf{v} \leftarrow \mathbf{u}/||\mathbf{u}||_2$ {Normalize orthogonal direction}
Define $g(\theta) =$ SOFTKENDALL($\mathbf{r}\cos(\theta) + \mathbf{v}\sin(\theta)$, $\mathbf{X}$, $\mathbf{y}$)
Phase 1: Grid Search
$\Theta \leftarrow \{0, \frac{2\pi}{G}, \frac{4\pi}{G}, \ldots, \frac{2\pi(G-1)}{G}\}$ {Grid points}
Evaluate $g(\theta)$ for all $\theta \in \Theta$
$\Theta_{\text{best}} \leftarrow$ top K angles with lowest $g(\theta)$ values
Phase 2: Local Refinement
$\theta^* \leftarrow \infty$, $f^* \leftarrow \infty$
for each $\theta_c \in \Theta_{\text{best}}$ **do**
  $\delta \leftarrow 2\pi/G$ {Bracket half-width}
  bracket $\leftarrow [\theta_c - \delta, \theta_c + \delta]$
  result $\leftarrow$ R's `optimize`(g, interval = bracket, tol = 10^{-8})
  if result.objective $< f^*$ **then**
    $\theta^* \leftarrow$ result.minimum
    $f^* \leftarrow$ result.objective
  end if
end for
Construct optimized reference point
$\mathbf{r}^* \leftarrow \mathbf{r}\cos(\theta^*) + \mathbf{v}\sin(\theta^*)$
$\mathbf{r}^* \leftarrow \mathbf{r}^*/||\mathbf{r}^*||_2$ {Renormalize for numerical stability}
return $\mathbf{r}^*$, f^*

4.14 Computational Performance Analysis

This section analyzes the computational characteristics of the spherical coordinate descent algorithm and compares its performance to alternative approaches.

4.14.1 Time Complexity Analysis

The algorithm's time complexity per iteration is now clearly dominated by the two-phase optimization procedure:

- **Phase 1 - Grid Search**: $O(G \cdot n^2) = O(64 \cdot n^2)$ for systematic exploration
- **Phase 2 - Local Refinement**: $O(K \cdot L \cdot n^2) = O(2 \cdot L \cdot n^2)$ where $L \approx 15$ is the average number of iterations for R's `optimize()`

- **Great circle construction**: $O(d)$
- **UCB selection**: $O(A)$

The total per-iteration complexity is $O((G + KL) \cdot n^2 + d + A) \approx O(94 \cdot n^2)$ since $(64 + 2 \cdot 15) = 94$ and $n^2 \gg d + A$ for our parameters.

4.14.2 Space Complexity

Memory requirements are modest:

- **Embedding storage**: $O(nd)$ for embedding matrix
- **Pairwise differences**: $O(n^2)$ if stored explicitly, $O(1)$ if computed on-demand
- **UCB statistics**: $O(d)$ for dimension-specific tracking
- **Grid evaluation storage**: $O(G) = O(64)$ for temporary storage during Phase 1
- **Optimization history**: $O(I_{\max})$ if full trajectory is stored

Total space complexity is $O(nd + n^2)$, which is acceptable for our problem sizes.

4.14.3 Convergence Rate Analysis

Empirical analysis of convergence behavior shows:

- **Initial rapid improvement**: Objective typically improves by $> 90\%$ in first 50 iterations due to effective global exploration
- **Linear convergence phase**: Steady improvement for iterations 50-200 as local refinement becomes dominant
- **Fine-tuning phase**: Slow convergence in final iterations, governed by tolerance parameters

Typical convergence occurs within 150-300 iterations, well below the maximum limit of 500.

4.14.4 Comparison with Pure Grid Search

The two-phase approach significantly outperforms pure grid search:

- **Pure grid search**: Limited by grid resolution, typically achieving 2-3 digits of accuracy
- **Two-phase approach**: Local refinement achieves 8-10 digits of accuracy
- **Computational cost**: Only 20-30% higher than pure grid search due to focused local optimization

4.14.5 *Scalability Considerations*

The algorithm's scalability is primarily limited by:

- **Sample size**: $O(n^2)$ scaling with training data size
- **Dimensionality**: Linear scaling with embedding dimension d
- **Grid resolution**: Linear scaling with G

For larger applications, potential optimizations include:

- **Stochastic variants**: Sample random pairs instead of all $O(n^2)$ pairs
- **Parallel grid evaluation**: Distribute Phase 1 grid search across multiple cores
- **Adaptive grid refinement**: Start with coarse grids and refine near optima
- **Warm-start local optimization**: Use grid search results to initialize more sophisticated local methods

4.15 Sensitivity Analysis and Robustness

Understanding the algorithm's sensitivity to hyperparameter choices and input variations is crucial for reliable deployment across different problem instances.

4.15.1 *Smoothing Parameter Sensitivity*

The soft Kendall's tau smoothing parameter σ critically affects optimization behavior:

- **Small** σ (< 0.01): Objective approaches classical Kendall's tau but becomes less smooth, making local optimization more difficult
- **Large** σ (> 0.1): Over-smoothing reduces correlation sensitivity and can mask important distinctions
- **Optimal range**: $\sigma \in [0.02, 0.08]$ provides good balance between smoothness and sensitivity
- **Adaptive selection**: Median-based adaptive selection generally performs well across diverse datasets

4.15.2 *Grid Resolution Sensitivity*

Grid search resolution affects global optimization quality:

- **Coarse grids** ($G < 32$): Risk missing optimal regions, particularly problematic for highly multi-modal objectives
- **Fine grids** ($G > 128$): Computational overhead with diminishing returns since local refinement handles precision
- **Recommended range**: $G \in [48, 96]$ balances coverage and efficiency
- **Adaptive strategies**: Could dynamically adjust grid resolution based on objective landscape roughness

4.15.3 Local Refinement Parameters

The number of candidates for local refinement significantly affects performance:

- **Single candidate** ($K = 1$): Faster but risks missing secondary optima
- **Multiple candidates** ($K \geq 3$): More thorough but diminishing returns beyond $K = 3$
- **Optimal choice**: $K = 2$ provides good balance for most objective landscapes

4.15.4 Active Set Size Impact

Active set management significantly affects convergence:

- **Small active sets** ($A < 256$): May miss important dimensions, particularly early in optimization
- **Large active sets** ($A > 768$): Reduced efficiency gains, approaching full coordinate cycling
- **Optimal sizing**: $A \approx d/3$ provides good performance/efficiency trade-off

4.15.5 Initialization Sensitivity

Algorithm performance varies with initialization strategy:

- **Random initialization**: Baseline performance, requires longer convergence
- **Data-driven initialization**: Using embeddings of extreme behavioral examples improves starting performance significantly
- **Multiple restarts**: Running 3-5 independent optimizations and selecting the best result improves robustness

4.15.6 *Robustness to Data Quality*

The algorithm's robustness to data quality issues:

- **Outliers**: Rank-based objective provides natural outlier resistance
- **Missing data**: Pairwise computation naturally handles missing behavioral outcomes
- **Small sample sizes**: Performance degrades gracefully with $n < 20$ observations
- **Noise**: Smoothed objective function provides some noise tolerance, though very high noise levels can overwhelm the signal

4.15.7 *Cross-Validation Performance*

Systematic cross-validation analysis shows:

- **Training performance**: Consistently achieves $\tau > 0.65$ on training data across multiple runs
- **Generalization**: Test performance typically within 0.05–0.10 of training performance
- **Stability**: Results consistent across different random splits and initialization seeds
- **Convergence reliability**: $> 95\%$ of runs converge to within 0.02 of the global optimum

4.16 Conclusion

The spherical coordinate descent algorithm provides a computationally tractable and theoretically sound approach to reference point optimization in high-dimensional embedding spaces. The method successfully navigates the challenges posed by the ultra-high dimensionality (1536 dimensions), multi-modal objective landscape, and complex constraint structure of the optimization problem.

Key algorithmic innovations include the great circle parameterization for maintaining spherical constraints, the two-phase optimization strategy combining systematic grid search with precise local refinement using R's `optimize()` function, and efficiency enhancements for scaling to high dimensions. The hybrid approach leverages the complementary strengths of global exploration and local precision, ensuring both robustness and accuracy.

The extensive hyperparameter analysis and sensitivity studies provide guidance for successful deployment across different problem instances, while the detailed computational analysis demonstrates the algorithm's practical scalability. The two-phase strategy's clear separation of global exploration and local refinement makes the algorithm both interpretable and debuggable.

The algorithm's strong empirical performance–achieving out-of-sample Kendall's tau correlations of 0.70 compared to 0.56 for naive baselines–demonstrates the practical value of systematic optimization for reference point discovery in the Reference-Anchored Trait Framework. The 23% improvement in correlation strength validates the sophisticated optimization approach and provides a solid foundation for behavioral prediction applications.

References

Aceves, P., & Evans, J. A. (2024). Mobilizing conceptual spaces: How word embedding models can inform measurement and theory within organization science. *Organization Science, 35*(3), 788–814.

Arora, S., Liang, Y., & Ma, T. (2017). *A simple but tough-to-beat baseline for sentence embeddings*. International Conference on Learning Representations.

Berger, J., Humphreys, A., Ludwig, S., Moe, W. W., Netzer, O., & Schweidel, D. A. (2022). Marketing insights from text analysis. *Marketing Letters, 33*(3), 389–415.

Cohen, J. (1988). *Statistical power analysis for the behavioral sciences* (2nd edn). Lawrence Erlbaum Associates, Hillsdale.

Falk, A., Becker, A., Dohmen, T., Huffman, D., & Sunde, U. (2023). The preference survey module: A validated instrument for measuring risk, time, and social preferences. *Management Science, 69*(4), 1935–1950.

Kendall, M. G. (1938). A new measure of rank correlation. *Biometrika, 30*(1/2), 81–93.

Mikolov, T., Chen, K., Corrado, G., & Dean, J. (2013). Efficient estimation of word representations in vector space. arXiv preprint arXiv:1301.3781

Mitchell, J., & Lapata, M. (2010). Composition in distributional models of semantics. *Cognitive Science, 34* (8), 1388–1429.

Park, K., Choe, Y. J., & Veitch, V. (2024). *The linear representation hypothesis and the geometry of large language models*. International Conference on Machine Learning.

Reimers, N., & Gurevych, I. (2019). Sentence-bert: Sentence embeddings using siamese bert-networks. In *Proceedings of the 2019 conference on empirical methods in natural language processing and the 9th international joint conference on natural language processing (EMNLP-IJCNLP)* (pp. 3982–3992).

Rodriguez, P. L., & Stewart, B. M. (2023). Embedding regression: Models for context-specific description and inference. *American Political Science Review, 117*(4), 1255–1274.

Vaswani, A., Shazeer, N., Parmar, N., Uszkoreit, J., Jones, L., Gomez, A. N., Kaiser, L., & Polosukhin, I. (2017). Attention is all you need. In *Advances in neural information processing systems* (pp. 5998–6008).

Zarifhonarvar, A., & Ganji, G. L. (2025). Understanding ai agents' decision-making: Evidence from risk and time preference elicitation. Working paper.

MIX
Papier aus verantwortungsvollen Quellen
Paper from responsible sources
FSC® C105338

If you have any concerns about our products,
you can contact us on
ProductSafety@springernature.com

In case Publisher is established outside the EU,
the EU authorized representative is:
Springer Nature Customer Service Center GmbH
Europaplatz 3, 69115 Heidelberg, Germany

Printed by Libri Plureos GmbH
in Hamburg, Germany